Dedicated to the memory of
Principal Kenneth Culbert,
educator who encouraged his students & community
to cherish each moment.

Acknowledgements:

We would like to extend our appreciation to all the contributors for sharing their memories of porches past as well as the role a porch might have in their lives today. With your enthusiasm and participation, we have expanded our original porch project into a more permanent keepsake of memories, past and present. In order to accomplish this, the students, teachers and community all joined to give valued support.

Several individuals deserve special mention:

The administration & faculty of Loudoun Valley High School, for providing support and supplies.

The US History students of Loudoun Valley High School, for providing photographs of Loudoun porches.

Dana B. Thompson for contributing her artistic talent, computer and design expertise.

Ashley George, a student at Loudoun Valley High School who volunteered many hours typing the manuscripts.

Leslie Bower for her creative force and enthusiasm.

Editor & Designer: L. Claire Kincannon
Associate Editors: Linda Ankrum & Marty Potts
Graphic Designer: Dana B. Thompson
Printer: Michael Healy, Better Impressions

©2005 Dancing Ink Press

All rights reserved under international and Pan-American copyright conventions. No part of this book may be used or reproduced in any manner whatsoever without written permission, except in the case of brief quotations embodied in critical articles or reviews. Each contributing author retains the right to his/her individual work.
Library of Congress Control Number: 2005904128
ISBN: 0-9726894-3-5
Inquires: dancingink@aol.com

What a joy it has been for me to participate in what began as a creative endeavor by teachers Linda Ankrum and Marty Potts to connect their students with the community's history. And now, we're *Rockin' with Porch Memories,* in words and pictures, including a broader spectrum of writers, poets and those individuals who hold dear the rich experience of life, past or present, on the uniquely American porch.

So, rock — shhhh —
listen to the corn growing —
chase the fireflies —
play hide-'n-seek —
"Alleee alleee in come freeee —"

Enjoy!

L. Claire Kincannon, editor

Jane Warren Norman on her porch at Longmoor near Purcellville, Virginia.

Porch memories & Perfor

Kenneth Culbert
Roger Blakeny
Michael Dolan
Lauren Smith
Robert M. Smith
Stuart Keefe
Gary Harris
Cynthia Dettmer
Justin Smith
Eric Fernandez
Johanna & Angie
Christian Amonson
Nicholas Wallaby
Luke Rochelle
Ruth & Virginia Tillett
Aledra Hollenbach

Nancy Serrano
Kayleigh Plamondan
Debbie Plamondan
Jeff Bowers
Greg Rickert
Edward Chamberlin
Grete Lenz
Marcia Hemminger
Jeremy Green
John Greene
Diane Budey
Ryan Baker
Kenzie Watson
Desirée Budesheim
Margot Watson
Scott Budesheim

nance

Students

at Loudoun Valley High School, Purcellville, Virginia cooperated in a cross curricular/cross community aural history project to examine the unique heritage of our region. A workshop was conducted by **Michael Dolan**, author of *The American Porch*, to teach the students the art of interviewing. Both English and History students catalogued community architecture, photographs, and oral recollections. Research into regional music performed on Loudoun porches encompassed the work of our music department. Drama students worked together with the music department in presenting a vignette of selected stories. This was shared with the community in an organized and advertised production.

Teachers *Marty Potts & Linda Ankrum*

Mr. Culbert's Story *as told to Ryan Baker*

As a child, Mr. Kenneth Culbert grew up with a porch on his house and put it to good use! Mr. Culbert was always playing war games, pretending he was a soldier. He loved to put himself out on the battlefield and pretend he was fighting for our country. He was born when World War II started, and his father was an officer in the U.S. Army. The porch was a base used by the kids, for war. He and his friends would always use the porch as a safe haven while fighting the other kids on the street. Before the game began, both teams would stock up on crab apples and fill their bases full of ammunition. Once both teams had their ammunition and were ready for battle, 'the war' would start. Crab apples flew from their sling shots and kids were dropping left and right. Once you were hit, the only way back into the game was if you were saved by one of the soldiers from your team and brought back to your base. This could go on for two to three hours a day!

But when the war was over for the day, and the kids were still ready for more action, they would spice things up by enticing Mr. Culbert's goat. That's right, the kids would throw things at the goat to get it to come after them and see if they could get onto the porch before getting rammed in the butt. It seemed that Mr. Culbert's little brother, Corky, was always a favorite target for the goat who was called Billy the Kid.

Mr. Culbert's Play

Characters:
    David "Corky" Culbert: Becca   Larry: Caleb   Puddleduck: Beth
    Kenny Culbert: Sarah   Hubert: Misa   Lemonade Girl #1: Carly
    Jimmy Culbert: Gabe   Frankie: Katey   Lemonade Girl #2: Meghan

Hubert: This is a reenactment of the war games played by Mr. Culbert and his friends during his childhood summer.
Kenny: I am so bored, what is there to do?
    (Neighbors approach. Katey picks up an apple and throws it at Sarah.)
Frankie: We declare war Kenny Culbert!!
Jimmy: You're dead meat Frankie!
    (Exit all but Sarah)
Kenny: When my friends and I were young, we used to play a little war game. Each team would pick a side of the porch, and then we'd throw crab apples back and forth, to get the opposing team members out. Usually we'd play for about two hours…then when we were completely out of energy…we'd play with the goat, Billy the Kid. Oh, looks like the game is startin' I better go!
    (Enter all with mud on face and soldier clothes)
Hubert: Team Captain 1!
Kenny: Team Captain 2!
Corky: Team Captain 3!
Frankie: Corky Culbert! *(Slaps Becca on the back of the head)* There are only two teams!
    (Misa chooses Caleb, Sarah chooses Beth, Misa chooses Katey, Sarah chooses Gabe, Sarah & Misa look at Becca.)
Hubert: You can have him.
Kenny: No, you can.
Hubert: I insist…
Kenny: I don't want him.
Hubert: He's too slow!
Kenny: He smells funny! *(Becca looks sad)*
Hubert: All right, I'll take him…*(To Becca)* you better not make us lose!
    (Run to different sides of the porch.)
Frankie: *(To Becca)* If you get OUT….run off the porch and wait for someone to bring you back into the game.
Corky: Let's start the war! Let's start the war!
    (Gabe throws apple at Becca. Everyone picks up apples and throws them.)
    (Katey stands up…everyone freezes)
Frankie: The neighbor boys and I used to play with crab apples. Nobody ever got hurt, seriously hurt, but sometimes Corky would run inside crying to his momma *(starts laughing)*.
    (Katey goes back to position…Becca stands up)
Corky: The guys used to always pick on me because I was the slowest one, but I liked tagging along with the big kids.

My Favorite Porch Memories

by Roger Blakeney

I loved to sit on the porch during a fall or spring rain, having to bundle up because the rain could bring a chill. The rain was soft and gentle, not harsh or threatening, and so aromatic – so fresh – so clean.

One day my friends and I were riding our bicycles. Mine was a Columbia with thick tires. As we rode by my front porch, I waved "hi" to my dad who was rocking in his old wooden rocker while he read the paper. Dad yelled back a "hi" which was filled with surprise because as he returned our salute, the old rocker exploded out from under him. We were laughing so hard that we could not control our bikes, and we proceeded to drive through the fence into the yard destroying our fence line. I still laugh when I think of that 'exploding chair'.

Roger Blakeney's Play

Characters:
- Roger Blakeney–present: Caleb
- Roger Blakeney–past: Gabe
- Girl # 1: Carly
- Girl # 2: Meghan
- Daddy: John
- Mommy: Becca

Roger present: I often like to look back to a certain memory of mine from my childhood. As I sit upon a porch and rock I remember…

(Memory sequence)

Roger past: Hey guys, let's look at my new Columbia bike.
Girl # 1: Wow, cool thick tires.
Girl # 2: And take a look at that shiny silver ringer too. *(Ding-Ding)*
Roger past: Uh huh. Lets go riding. I want to try out these new tires here.

(End Sequence)

Roger present: Those were good times, the wind in your hair, the smell of rubber as you squealed to a stop and spent a penny for a piece of gum.

(Memory sequence)

Meghan: This here new gum is mighty fine.
Girl # 1: Yeah, it is. Why don't you give me some?
Girl # 2: No way! It cost me a whole penny.
Girl # 1: Hey Rog, why don't we head back to your house?
Roger past: Ok, my ma should have a fresh pitcher of lemonade made by now.

(End sequence)

Roger present: Those were the days. Fresh iced lemonade on my big front porch.

(Memory sequence)

Girl # 1: Hi Mister Blakeney. How are you today?
Roger past: Don't bother father, he's reading the newspaper. Trying to understand the world or something.
Girl # 2: Look the lemonade is ready. Thanks Miz Blakeney.
Roger past: Thanks ma.
Girl # 1: This is so good Rog, how does your ma do it?
Roger past: I don't know. Hey, how about we go out ridin' again?
Girl # 2 & Girl # 1: Sure.
Roger past: Lets go then.

(End sequence)

Roger present: I can still remember how that day we left the porch, mounted our bikes and began to leave the yard.

(Memory sequence)

Roger past: Bye pa.

(John's father raises hand and waves as children peddle off. (Boom!!!!) Looking back over their shoulder they hear loud noise and then see Roger's father's rocker explode).

(End sequence)

Roger present: *(chuckle)* That was a strange day…very amusing though. Right after my father's chair broke, my friends and I were laughing so hard that we ended up running over my mother's flower garden and then hitting the white picket fence head on. Even to this day, the memory of my father's exploding chair still brings tears of laughter to my eyes.

how the Coffin *wound up on our porch*

by Michael Dolan

My family and I live at the edge of Washington, D.C., in an old streetcar neighborhood called Palisades. Save for a sprinkling of ramblers, and unfortunately, ever more tract-mansion monstrosities, Palisades consists of ranks of bungalows and four-squares, nearly all with porches. Some porches, like ours used to be, are enclosed in jalousies, some remade into rooms, others are outfitted in the classic style with gliders and wicker and benches and fans and the other amenities of porch life.

As far as I know, only one porch in Palisades includes among its furnishings a coffin.

The coffin is my own, custom-carpentered to fit my frame, though, in a pinch, it would accommodate someone slightly larger. Although I don't expect to use it in the proper way anytime soon, my coffin sits by the front door, loaded not only with intimations of mortality but, most of the time, with hockey sticks, Frisbees, baseball gloves, badminton rackets, soccer shin guards, and so forth.

The coffin came to our porch because of the one night a year that we empty it of sports gear. We're semi-devout Catholics, but our liturgical calendar has an additional holy day of obligation: October 31. At our house, Halloween is an immovable feast. Before we had our son, Marty, Eileen and I would decorate the porch with candlelit pumpkins. For a while, we grew them in the backyard. They sprouted from seeds cast into the compost heap that produced weird mutant fruit the size of babies' skulls. One year, a bumper crop left the porch steps decorated with some twenty tiny pumpkins with their leering grins.

But Marty's arrival on October 23, 1989, seriously cut into our pumpkin-carving. And, as he grew and absorbed his parents' enthusiasm for the eve of All Saints' Day, Marty developed his own ideas about how to celebrate Halloween. One year, the kids across the street hammered together crude crosses and staked out an imitation cemetery. The following autumn, Marty, who had just turned four, announced that he wanted a graveyard in the front yard, like the one Sam and Katy had put up.

"Well, how can we do that?" I asked.

"Uncle Chris!" he chirped. Uncle Chris, Eileen's youngest brother, runs a company that builds theatrical scenery. He also makes first-rate furniture. Later that week, he happened to stop by.

"Chris, I need to make a graveyard," Marty said, "for Halloween"

"Marty," Chris said. "if you can think it up, you can make it at my shop."

So on the eve of All Hallow's Eve, 1993, Marty and I visited Chris' shop down in Lorton, Virginia. We sawed. We routed – well, Chris and I sawed and routed. I indulge my child, but not to the extent of letting a four-year-old use power tools. Marty and I came home with a stack of fake tombstones sporting winged skulls, the message "RIP" and sundry other ghoulish images.

The faux bone yard was a big hit. We stowed the crosses and tombstones in the basement, figuring they'd constitute the annual display. But the next fall, after his birthday party, Marty said he wanted to take it a step further.

"I want a coffin," he said.

"Call Uncle Chris."

Once again, Marty and I trekked down to the shop, where Chris had interrupted work on a rush job for ABC-TV to clamp a couple of sheets of 3/4-inch plywood to one another atop a pair of sawhorses. He pointed to me.

"Jump up," he said, pointing a carpenter's pencil at me. I jumped up and arranged myself on the plywood. Chris sketched the outline of my corpse, er, body.

"Okay" he said. "Now get out of the way. I haven't got time for you to help me."

The next 90 minutes were a blur of radial saw cuts and power driver jabs, as Chris cut away everything that wasn't coffin and assembled the pieces into a classic box-narrow at the feet, wide at the shoulders, angled in again at the head. Using a piano hinge, he attached the lid, wiped the entire rig with a coat of stain, then let me rout a quick "RIP" into it.

"Try it on," he said. "I gotta get back to work."

I climbed into the box and crossed my hands over my chest. Chris and Marty lowered the lid. It fitted with startling precision; only a thin rind of light showed through. Marty pronounced the coffin excellent, I climbed out, and we loaded it into the Explorer, leaving Chris to finish his set for *Nightline*.

Back home, we arranged the coffin on the lawn as the centerpiece of the graveyard, running a trouble light into it and propping the lid open with a bloodied rubber hand. The effect was delightfully alarming.

The next night, our house drew more than the usual stream of trick-or-treaters. People drove and hiked to our block specifically to see the coffin, have their pictures taken standing beside, even getting inside. But Halloween only lasts one night. Afterwards we had to figure out what to do with a 75-lb., 6'10" plywood coffin the other 364 nights of the year. We tried storing it in the basement, but there wasn't room. Fortunately, a neighbor with a bigger house let us haul it into his basement – until he decided to renovate.

There was really only one spot we could store the gloomy prop, on our renovated front porch. Instead of resembling a sanatorium for aged wicker and rust ridden gliders, it sparkled and gleamed–not exactly the place for a coffin, but there it was. The first week in November 1999, Marty and I took down the Halloween display and, instead of hiding the coffin, we installed it on the porch and filled it with sports equipment.

Ever since, there it's been – in winter a fine place to rack firewood and stack kindling, in spring a warm spot on which to put sun-hungry houseplants, in summer a south-facing surface on which to dry bathing suits and towels wet from the pool.

And every autumn, when Marty's birthday signals the official start of Halloween, we empty the coffin and put it out in the yard with the rest of the stuff – a symbol of death that, at our house anyway, has become part of life.

The Coffin Play

Characters:
    Mary Sue: Moriah   Marty: Andrew   Uncle Chris: Robbie
    Amanda Jane: Vanessa   Big Sis, Danny: Lynn

SCENE 1:

(Mary Sue and Amanda Jane walking in stage right. They look into the audience. Curtain is closed.)

Mary Sue: Wow looks good, what do you think?
Amanda Jane: Best on the block, lets go see what Marty's looks like.

(Curtain opens. Girls walk across stage toward Marty and his jack-o-lantern. Girls are laughing and giggling.)

Amanda Jane: Hey Marty. *(Laughing behind their back)*
Mary Sue: Nice...
Amanda Jane: Pumpkins...Ha ha *(Laughing harder)*
Marty: What's wrong with them?
Mary Sue: Well....
Both Girls: Look at your yard and look at our yard.

(Laughing, pointing towards audience.)

Marty: Wow! A graveyard. *(Excited at first then hangs his head)* Well mine's not done yet.

(Girls still laughing very hard)

Well look, you guys are a bunch of...of...DUMB-HEADS.

(Laughing to himself looking proud of telling them what he thought of them)

Mary Sue: Dumb-heads? *(Laughing very hard)*
Amanda Jane: That's like soooo kindergarten.
Marty: Well....you guys better get out of here or I'll, I'll...beat you up.

(Danny walks right behind him with a mean grin. Girls see Danny and they scream and run)

Marty: Yeah...Look at me I'm so tuff. *(Flexing muscles)*

(Danny taps him on shoulder. Marty screams. Then sighs with relief, with look of terror still on his face.)

Oh it's just you Danielle.
Danny: It's Danny. *(very foreboding)*
Marty: Right, right I know.
Danny: So what are those brats bagging you about this time.
Marty: Our Halloween decorations suck, and they have a whole graveyard and everything.
Danny: You're such a twerp. Just ask Uncle Chris to make you a stupid graveyard. Now go call him.

(Brother and sister stand, walk toward house, Danny pushes Marty through door)

SCENE 2:

(Curtain is closed. Marty is stage left in front of curtain with spotlight on him and phone. He dials. Phone rings. Spotlight comes up on Uncle Chris stage right in front of curtain. He picks up phone)

Marty: Hi Uncle Chris. It's Marty.
Uncle Chris: Hey Marty! How ya doin kid?
Marty: Well, I need a coffin.
Uncle Chris: *(Smirks at his nephew's request, but looks slightly confused)* A coffin?
Marty: It's for Halloween to show up the little girls next door.
Uncle Chris: Ohhh well then...
Marty: I need to make my yard look awesome.
Uncle Chris: Well what do you need?
Marty: Ok, a coffin, and some tombstones, and some......*(Lights and voices fade)*

(You hear sawing, hammering, drilling, basic tool noises, then a loud crash and a loud OW!)
(Spotlight comes up on Uncle Chris on right stage in front of curtain, dirty, and an obvious bandage on one of his fingers. He walks to the phone and with some trouble he dials it. A phone rings and a spotlight comes up on Marty answering the phone)

Marty: Hello.
Uncle Chris: Hey Marty.
Marty: *(excitedly)* Hey Uncle Chris, Happy Halloween!
Uncle Chris: It's all ready. I'll bring it over in a while. *(Black Out)*

SCENE 3: *(Black-light lights the scene.*

There is a tree with a man tied to the top and a rope to pull and make him drop. Two fake piles of dirt next to, two gravestones with Mary Sue on one and Amanda Jane on the other. A coffin is on one side of the stairs, closed. Jack-o-lanterns are all around the yard. Eerie music is playing and fog covers most of the ground. Mary Sue and Amanda Jane enter in angel costumes looking for Marty and getting spooked by the scene)

Mary Sue: *(looking at the graves)* Yeah..
Amanda Jane: Right..
Both: He wishes.
Mary Sue: Where..
Amanda Jane: Is he?
Mary Sue: Anyways. *(looking around and backing off stage holding hands)*
Amanda Jane: I hate to...
Mary Sue: Say it...
Amanda Jane: But...
Both: I'm scared.

(They turn, run and come face to face with Marty dressed as monster. Strobe lights flash. They scream, run toward other side of stage. Dummy falls, still dangling from tree. They scream, try to run around it, but Uncle Chris dressed as axe murderer or grim reaper or something to that affect, blocks their path. They scream, run to middle of stage, hug, look frantically around, back up slowly)

Mary Sue: I!
Amanda Jane: Wanna!
Mary Sue: Go!
Both: HOME!!!!!!

(They back into coffin. It pops open and Danny, dressed as vampire sits up, grabs both screaming girls. Danny pulls girls into coffin and shuts lid. They free themselves and run screaming through audience and out back of auditorium.)

SCENE 4:

(Marty enters, dressed normally, in front of curtain)

Marty: That was the best Halloween ever! Mary Sue and Amanda Jane never bothered me again. I was king of the neighborhood! Now where did I put my baseball?

(He looks around, pats clothes as curtain opens. House back to normal. Coffin rests on front porch. Marty digs through coffin, tossing out sports equipment. Danny enters, picks up discarded bat.)

Marty: *(finding the ball)* There it is!
(He turns around to see Danny and jumps in fright)

Danny: Ready to go squirt?

Marty: *(voice slightly shaking)* Yeah.

(They walk down the proch steps and head off right. Marty stops at the edge of the curtain)

Marty: *(to audience)* Well, maybe not king of the neighborhood.
(motions to where his sister just walked off)

Danny: *(very harsh voice)* COME ON!!!

(Marty jumps up and runs after her.)

Porch Conversation

Robert M. Smith as interviewed by Lauren Smith

What was the most dramatic event that happened to you on your porch?
"My cousin Joe-Joe once fell off the porch and almost bit his tongue off. He had to get stitches. He was just sitting on the rail, lost his balance, and fell off backwards. We were very worried when it first happened, but when he got back from the hospital we all just laughed at him!"

What was the most sentimental memory that happened on your porch?
"Sitting on the porch, rocking on the chair with my Nonna (grandmother). It was a big rocking chair with thick wooden boards for armrests. My sister and I were small enough that we use to sit, one on each side of the rocking chair. My Nonna would rock the chair and my sister and I would rock with her and say 'Nooooooonna…' for hours straight every single day. It was great!"

What was the funniest memory you have had on your porch?
"When I was about four years old, my Uncle Baisel told me to go down to the store and buy him a pack of cigarettes. He said that if I did, that he would give me a nickel (back then, cigarettes were twenty cents a pack). So I got them for him. He was waiting on the porch for me to get back. I handed him the nickel change, and his pack of cigarettes. He stuck the nickel in his pocket and just looked at me. I said, 'what about my nickel' and Uncle Baisel said to me, 'Ha Ha! I tricked you! I wasn't' going to give you the nickel!' So I looked up at him and said 'Fine! Keep your F%#@ing nickel!' Everyone was shocked, but then again he *did* promise me that nickel. And so he did."

What was the most character defining moment you had on your porch?
"We were down at the last porch on my street and my cousin Joe-Joe and I were talking to my cousin's friend Wyonita. She was a Mexican girl, about fourteen years old. Joe-Joe was about fourteen too, and I was ten. Well, they were both making fun of me and I said something to Wyonita that she didn't like, so she grabbed her brush, the one she just finished brushing her hair with, and threw it at me. I picked it up and threw it as hard as I could at her. She didn't catch it and it went through the window into her house. Everyone goes, "Oh Bobby…you're gonna have to tell her Mom!" and then everyone ran away, and I was all by myself. I went up to the door and knocked. It felt like I waited forever for her mother to come to the door. I just stood there waiting, scared out of my mind. I could have run away, but I didn't. And that helped build my character. It taught me not to run from my fears, but to confront them."

What was your most serene or peaceful moment on your porch?
"Sitting on the porch listening to the spring rain. Or when the snow fell and I would watch it twirl down from the sky. It was so amazing because I was outside in it, not just inside watching. The best was when I would go out on my porch to pick up the ice cold, freshly delivered milk or the freshly squeezed orange juice that sat outside waiting for someone to bring it in. Those were the days."

What was the most fun that you had on your porch?
"My grandmother used to baby-sit my sister and me sometimes. When my sister and I got too rowdy she used to lock my sister in her room. I used to go out on the porch and wait for my grandmother to leave. As soon as she was out of sight, I would climb up the drainage pipe onto the roof of the porch and climb into my sister's room. We'd be up there playing and when we got loud, I would see the door open, and my grandmother would walk in the room. I jumped out the window, ran across the roof, slid down the drainage pipe, and into the house, acting like I was there the whole time."

The Nickel Play

Characters:
- Narrator: Erin Conroy
- Mary Sue: Biz Sperduto
- Betsy: Kati Cutshall
- Twinkie: Amanda Mouser
- Aunt: Kristen Kelley
- Uncle: Anthony Elworthy
- Chinese Storeowner: Alex Seebeck

(Mary Sue, Betsy, and Twinkie sit on edge of front porch; legs dangling. All are wearing little girl dresses and saddle shoes with white socks. Mary Sue and Betsy have one Popsicle each; Twinkie has two and is licking violently. Aunt is sweeping the porch in her apron. Twinkie finishes her Popsicle and looks around at the other girls eating. She takes Mary Sue's Popsicle and starts eating it. Mary Sue looks frustrated.)

Narrator: It was another hot summer morning in Virginia. Mary Sue, Betsy, and Twinkie were sitting on the front porch, trying to cool off.

Aunt: You girls better not drip any of that on your dresses, ya hear?

All Girls: Yes Ma'am.

Narrator: But this Saturday morning was a bit different. Mary Sue's uncle had a special plan for the girls.

Uncle: You girls head on down to the general store and get me a packa' cigarettes.

Twinkie: Does that mean we have to walk?

Mary Sue: Yes Twinkie, we gotta walk.

Betsy: But we are eating our Popsicles!

Uncle: I'll give you a nickel each if ya do it!

Mary Sue: All right uncle, we'll get em' for ya.

Aunt: You all come straight back here now. Don't be talking to strangers.

All Girls: Yes Ma'am.

Narrator: So the girls set off. Twinkie tried her hardest to keep up.

(At store, Chinese storeowner is mumbling to himself and very grumpy!)

Mary Sue: Hello sir. I was wondering if we could get a pack a' cigarettes for my uncle.

Chinese Storeowner: *(grumbling)* Oh maan. I no want to get dem. Dey on high sheff. Make fat frien get dem. She nee exercise. Hwa hwa hwa hwa hwa hwa. *(Reaches up to high shelf, looks around shoulder and sees Twinkie eating all of his free candy. Gets mad!)* You take ONE fat girl!! He you do. Da 25 cen. Have nice Daaayyy! Don feed fat frien, hwa hwa.

Betsy: Thank ya sir.

(All girls are leaving, storeowner says, in the background)

Storeowner: Wife numba fo', you make rice cake.

Narrator: And so, cigarettes in hand, the girls headed home, excited about getting their money.

Mary Sue: We got em for ya uncle! *(long pause)* Umm sir....

Betsy: Can we have our nickels?

Twinkie: Yeahhh! And some food too, that walk made me hungry!

Uncle: Ha ha ha ha, I tricked you! I'm not giving you girls nothin! *(Snaps suspenders)*

(Girls look at each other getting angrier and angrier. All cross their arms, Twinkie tries too...)

Narrator: The porch drama intensified...

Mary Sue: *(in deep and quiet anger)* FINE! *(Then gets high pitched and angry)* Keep your *(mouths bad word while loud beep sounds)* nickel!!

Betsy: YEAH!!

(Everyone exchanges surprised ad horrified glances. Aunt and uncle look very angry. But, as they make eye contact, begin to smile.)

Uncle: hahahaha, ok ok, I'll give you girls your money.

Narrator: And so the evening on the porch came to an end. The girls got their money, and Twinkie stayed for dinner. The girls continued to make mischief, eat Popsicles and grow in many ways. Especially Twinkie.

Interviews from the porches of Lovettsville

interviewers: Justin Smith & Eric Fernandez

"We had a large porch with high railings and large white posts. The most memorable part of our porch was the large painted wooden steps. There were three or four of them. My sister was about seven and we were playing some silly game. She and I were jumping off the top of the steps down to the concrete walkway. Well, my sister jumped, but she must have tripped 'cause she smacked her kneecap on the third step. I remembering hearing a loud pop. Then I ran to get my mother and she eventually took her to the hospital. After a few hours we found out she shattered her kneecap. It was a long time before she could walk up or down those steps again."

Johanna

"I remember when my father told me about how his older sister jumped off their second story porch. My father said 'I told her I would catch her, but I didn't.' He remembers being at the hospital for hours. His sister broke her leg in two places."

Angie

interviewer: Stuart Keefe

"It was late afternoon, a blue jay went into the tree and knocked a bat out of the tree then it fell to the ground. I thought it was a bird but when I looked closer, it was a red bat with three babies attached. I picked it up with a pool skimmer and put it in a shoe box then cut open the side. I left it there over night and in the morning it was gone. I called rescue league and they said that this was a common occurrence. They said that blue jays attack mother bats and that mother bats cannot fly when on the ground. They must be hanging to take off in flight."

Gary Harris

"I've enjoyed sitting on my back porch, visiting with my next-door neighbors and watching their little girls grow up."

Cynthia Dettmer

Interview from a porch in Philomont

interviewer: Christian Amonson

"When I was young, my family did not own any land. We lived on the third floor of a rundown tenement house in Richmond. As children, my brothers and I had no place to play but the street. We had no land of our own. I learned hard work and perseverance from my father, and after many years of labor, I was able to buy this old house and the land that it rests on. That was twenty years ago. I love to sit on this porch with my wife (and sometimes the grandchildren too) and watch the sun set. From here, I can see the five acres that we worked so hard for. I am filled with pride, and yet humbled every time I set foot out the front door. I know my father is looking down from Heaven onto this porch with a big smile on his face. I think he is proud too."

Nicholas Wallaby

Interviews from the porches of Hamilton

interviewer: Luke Rochelle

What is your fondest memory on the porch?

Sisters,
Ruth & Virginia Tillett: Stated that they had many family gatherings on their porch before their parents passed away.

Aledra Hollenbach: Having their children play soccer on the porch . . . Retriever dog playing on the porch . . . Also, their children used to play under the porch.

Nancy Serrano: When they were getting ready for Hamilton Days. Because she was looking around and no one was up, the sun was coming up and it looked really nice.

What is your worst memory on the porch?

Ruth & Virginia Tillett: Finding out that their mother's health was failing.

Aledra Hollenbach: When they had to carry their dog up the steps (bad health).

Nancy Serrano: When they renovated the porch, the Hamilton Committee was angry that they built a garage.

What changes have you seen happen in Hamilton from your porch?

Ruth & Virginia Tillett: A lot more traffic. Their father owned 75 acres of farmland in Hamilton which was sold to a builder who built the newer homes in Hamilton. Seeing all the happy kids play at the Hamilton playground.

Aledra Hollenbach: The house sits on a road where many people walk past, so they would get into a lot of conversations with the passers-by.

Interviews from the porches of Lucketts

interviewer: Kayleigh Plamondan

"My dad and I were sitting on our porch out in Lucketts one day. There is a road at the top of the hill straight ahead and then a creek at the bottom, next to our driveway. One day we saw at least one-hundred pigs running down the hill and then across our driveway. My dad and I grabbed our pellet guns and just started shooting at them. It was so much fun."

Jeff Bowers, neighbor

"When I was young, we used to sit on my grandmother's screened porch and play all day long while the grown-ups talked inside. We would wait until dinner was ready, then we would all sit down to eat inside. When we were done, we would race back out to the porch and play until it was time to go home. I always had a good time."

Debbie Plamondan, mother of Kayleigh

Interviews from the porches of Waterford

interviewer: Greg Rickert and Grete Lenz

"The porch on the side of my house serves as a viewpoint of a large chunk of the yard. It also is a place to sit back, relax, and play the ukelele on a hot summer day. It has a few wooden chairs, a table, and a sofa. The view of Clarke's Gap Road is spectacular! Once, the porch was featured on a Hechinger's commercial, along with my dog, Chester. This infamous commercial debuted on TV back when I was a youngster in Waterford Elementary School.

My porch is a sacred place, both to me and my rowdy neighbors on Clarke's Gap."

Edward Chamberlin

"I love sitting on my front porch in Waterford, Virginia. On summer mornings, as the sun peeks over the mountains to the east, I enjoy basking in the new day's warmth with a cup of freshly brewed coffee in my hand. I can hear the gentle mooing of cows in a nearby pasture, the Canada geese honking as they fly overhead, and the bees buzzing as they pollinate the azaleas surrounding this porch. I love the feel of the gentle breeze that makes the porch cool in the early morning, savoring it for soon the temperatures will be high. As I read the morning paper, I can gaze over the serene view of fields dotted with animals, crops, and a few homes. Nothing is more relaxing than spending some time on my Waterford porch."

Marcia Hemminger

Interviews from the porches of Round Hill

interviewer: Jeremy Green

"My grandfather built the porch in our backyard when I was only a toddler. My brother and I would leap off the rail to the ground. I thought my brother had broken his leg one time. On a hot, sunny day, the only shade we could find was under the porch. That porch is still there today."

John Greene

"The only thing we had resembling a porch was a step in front of the door. There wasn't much to it except an old rug and a few dead rats. The rest of the house, if you could call it that, was in the same pitiful condition. I cannot recall any good memories about it. Quite the opposite. It was the entrance to my miserable life."

Diana Budey

Interviews from the porches of Other Places

interviewers: Kenzie Watson and Desiree Budesheim

"During the summer, my family would go out to visit my grandmother. She had a big porch painted white with rocking chairs and a coffee table that always had some type of candy on it. My brother, sister and I used to sleep outside on the porch. Those were the best times of my life. The crickets would quietly chirp, and the waves would softly crash upon the ocean, lulling us to sleep."

Margot Watson, porch in Canox, British Columbia, Canada

"Every year, we made it a point to visit my mother who lived in Arizona, so she could see how our family was doing. She had a huge porch that overlooked her pool and a lot of her land. When the sun would set we would sit on the porch and drink cool lemonade."

Scott Budesheim, porch in Phoenix, Arizona

Porches in Prose

Russell Baker • Michelle Y. Green

Sharyn McCrumb • Frank Raflo

excerpt from *Growing Up*

by Russell Baker

Morrisonville was a poor place to prepare for a struggle with the twentieth century, but delightful place to spend a childhood. It was a summer day drenched with sunlight, fields yellow with buttercups, and barn lofts sweet with hay. Clusters of purple perfumed the air from the great vine enclosing the end of my grandmother's porch, and wild roses covered the fences.

On a broiling afternoon when the men were away at work and all the women napped, I moved through majestic depths of silences, silences so immense I could hear the corn growing. Under these silences there was an orchestra of natural music playing notes no city child would ever hear. A certain crackle from the henhouse meant we had gained an egg. The creak of a porch swing told of a momentary breeze blowing across my grandmother's yard. Moving past Liz Virts's barn as quietly as an Indian, I could hear the swish of a horse's tail and knew the horseflies were out in strength. As I tiptoed along a mossy bank to surprise a frog, a faint splash told me the quarry had spotted me and slipped into the stream. Wandering among the sleeping houses, I learned that with time roofs crackle under the power of the sun, and when I tired and came to my grandmother's house, I padded into her dark cool living room, lay flat on the floor and listened to the hypnotic beat of her pendulum clock on the wall ticking the meaningless hours away.

I was enjoying the luxuries of a rustic nineteenth century boyhood, but for the women Morrisonville life had few rewards. Both my mother and grandmother kept house very much as women did before the Civil War. It was astonishing that they had any energy left, after a day's work to nourish their mutual disdain. Their lives were hard, endless dirty labor. They had no electricity, gas, plumbing, or central heating. No refrigerator, no radio, no telephone, no automatic laundry, no vacuum cleaner. Lacking in-door toilets, they had to empty sour, and fumigate each morning, the noisome slop jars which sat in bedrooms during the night.

For baths, laundry and dishwashing they hauled buckets of water from a spring at the foot of a hill. To heat it, they chopped kindling to fire their wood stoves. They boiled laundry in tubs, scrubbed it on washboards until knuckles were raw, and wrung it out by hand. Ironing was a business of lifting, heaving metal weights heated on top of the stove.

They scrubbed floors on hands and knees, thrashed rugs with carpet beaters, killed and plucked their own chickens, baked bread, and pastries, grew and canned their own vegetables, patched the family's clothing on treadle-operated sewing machines, deloused the chicken coops, preserved fruits, picked potato bugs and tomato worm to protect their garden crop, darned stockings, made jelly and relishes, rose before the men to start the stove for breakfast and pack lunch pails, polished the chimneys of kerosene lamps, and even found time to tend the geraniums, hollyhocks, nasturtiums, dahlias, and peonies that grew around every house. By the end of a summer day a Morrisonville woman had toiled like a serf.

At sundown the men drifted back from the fields exhausted and steaming. They scrubbed themselves in enamel basins and, when supper was eaten, climbed on to Ida Rebecca's porch to watch the night arrive. Presently the women joined them, and the twilight music of Morrisonville began.

The swing creaking, rocking chairs whispering on the porch planks, voices murmuring approval of the sagacity of Uncle Irvey as he quietly observed for probably the ten-thousandth time in his life, "A man works from sun to sun, but woman's work is never done."

Ida Rebecca, presiding over the nightfall from the cane rocker, announcing, upon hearing of some woman "up there along the mountain" who had dropped dead hauling milk to the creamery, that "man is born to toil, and woman is born to suffer."

The timelessness of it: Nothing new had been said on that porch for a hundred years. If one of the children threw a rock close to someone's window, Uncle Harry removed his farmer's straw hat, swabbed the liner with his blue bandana, and spoke the wisdom of the ages to everyone's complete satisfaction by declaring, "Satan finds work for idle hands to do."

If I interrupted the conversation with a question, four or five adults competed to be the first to say, "Children are meant to be seen and not heard."

If one of my aunts mentioned the gossip about some woman "over there around Bollington" or "out there towards Hillsboro," she was certain to be silenced by a scowl from Ida Rebecca or Uncle Irvey and a reminder that "little pitchers have big ears."

I was listening to a conversation that had been going on for generations. Someone had a sick cow. The corn was "burning up" for lack of rain.

If the sheriff had arrested a local boy for shooting somebody's bull: "That boy never brought a thing but trouble to his mother, poor old soul."

Old Mr. Cooper, farms out there around Wheatland, had got his arm caught in the threshing machine and it had to be taken off, "poor old soul."

Ancient Aunt Zell who lived "down there around Lucketts," had to be buried on a day "so hot the flowers all wilted before they could get her in the ground, poor old soul."

When the lamps were lit inside, someone was certain to say to the children, "Early to bed and early to rise makes a man healthy, wealthy and wise."

Uncle Harry usually led the departures for he lived outside Morrisonville proper and had to walk a half-mile to get home. Only a year younger than Uncle Irvey, he was Ida Rebecca's quiet son. A dour man in sweat-stained work shirts, baggy trousers held up by yellow galluses, he worked in the fields, did some carpentry, turned up on a building job occasionally. He was gray, solemn, and frosty. A lonely man. His wife had died in childbirth twenty years earlier.

I knew he was slightly scandalous. Lately he had taken an interest in a younger woman who had borne an illegitimate child and been abandoned by her lover. Everybody knew Uncle Harry had "gone to housekeeping" with her and was devoted to her child, but he did not bring either mother or daughter to sit on Ida Rebecca's porch. Morrisonville's social code was rigid about such things.

Another person who did not join our evening assemblies was Annie Grisby, Ida Rebecca's next-door neighbor. Anne had been born in slavery, and this made her a notable citizen. Her log house was pointed out to travelers as one of the Morrisonville sights not to be ignored. "Anne was born in slavery," the visitor was always advised.

"Born in slavery." That phrase was uttered as though it were an incredible accomplishment on Annie's part. Elsewhere people boasted of neighbors who had tamed lightening, invented the wind-up Victrola, and gone aloft in flying machines, but we in Morrisonville didn't have to hang our heads. We had Annie. "Born in slavery." My mother told me about Abraham Lincoln, a great man who freed the slaves, and living so close to Annie, who had been freed by Lincoln himself, made me feel in touch with the historic past.

About the Author: *Russell Baker is one of the most distinguished practitioners of the personal-political essay in the English language. He was born in rural Morrisonville, Virginia in August, 1925. His early upbringing was not conducive to the development of the elegant, urbane literary style and trenchant criticism of contemporary city life he was to indulge in later. One of his earliest memories was of being nosed in his crib by an inquisitive cow. There were some pleasant memories of growing up close to nature: "summer days drenched in sunlight, fields yellow with buttercups." However, it was not a very progressive community; Baker's father, a stonemason, died of untreated diabetes when the boy was five, even though insulin had been discovered nearly a decade earlier. Baker's mother, trained as a schoolteacher, had studied for a year in college and encouraged her son's aptitude for language.*

Willie Pearl: Under the Mountain
by Michelle Y. Green

Chapter Two

Saturday morning couldn't come soon enough for Willie Pearl. After weeks and weeks of waiting, she would not be put off any longer. Johnny had to keep his promise today — or else. But first, there were chores to do. In the coal camps, a layer of gritty, black soot settled on everything. It was Willie Pearl's job to keep the front porch, the stone steps and the boardwalk to their neighbor's house swept clean. During the week a once-over with the corn broom was enough. But on Sundays, nothing less than a full scrubbing would do.

"Make sure it's clean enough for the Preacher to eat Sunday dinner off of," insisted Ma Rainey. Reverend Webb seemed to find his way up to the Mahone house for Sunday chicken and dumplings more times than not. Papa joked that the only thing left when Reverend Webb finished eating Ma's 'gospel bird' was the feet and the beak.

Willie Pearl struck the floorboards again and again with the corn broom. Clouds of coal dust flew. Next, she plunged the broom into a waiting pail of hot, soapy water. Billows of suds covered the front porch and the tops of her brown laced boots. Nearly done, Willie Pearl's excitement rose like the soap bubbles that drifted beyond the porch front.

Johnny was busy laying in coal from the coal shed out back. Tomorrow was Sunday, so he had to be sure there would be enough to keep the coal stove going for two days. There was lump coal for the cookstove in the kitchen, and slack coal to bank the fire in the front room. Chunk after chunk of the precious black ore tumbled into the coal scuttle. From the front porch, Willie Pearl strained to hear the sound of Johnny's shovel scraping across the coalhouse floor. As long as she heard him working, Willie Pearl knew Johnny was still around. She couldn't take the chance that he might forget — or worse — slip off on purpose.

"Yoo-hoo, illie Way earl Pay . . . Would you like to come over and lay-pay ith-way e-may?" Mae Ella's pig latin was terrible, but good enough for Willie Pearl to understand the Mae Ella was inviting her over to play. illie-Way earl-Pay yelled back to the porch several houses away.

"Not today, Mae Ella . . . I mean ae-Mae lla-Eay." Mae Ella's name was nearly impossible to pronounce in pig latin. "Ot-nay oday-tay–not today." Then feeling she owed her best friend some kind of explanation, Willie Pearl added, "too much work." A twinge of guilt hit Willie Pearl. She hadn't meant to lie, especially to her best friend. "just want her to be surprised when she sees what I've got," Willie Pearl said to herself, figuring that was a good enough reason. Willie Pearl tried her best to get back to work, but Mae Ella was not going to give up so easily.

"I thought we could walk down to Jenkins Theatre and catch the new Hoot Gibson feature," Mae Ella persisted. "Aunt Vera gave me 11 cents for my ticket."

Willie Pearl stopped working and leaned on her soapy broom. "It's not every day that a new Hoot Gibson feature comes to town, she thought. "And maybe I could borrow some of the money from Johnny . . . ." But thinking of Johnny only reminded her of her own important plans.

"No, thank you just the same," Willie Pearl decided with a firm swish of her broom.

"I'll let you hold my popcorn . . . ." Mae Ella was one girl who was used to getting her own way. But on this day, she was no match for Willie Pearl.

"Maybe next time," came the determined reply. The front door to Miss Vera's house slammed hard enough to be heard clear across the holler, and Mae Ella stomped inside. Willie Pearl tossed the rest of the soapy water across the porch, then ran out back to get the rinse water. It was only then she noticed -- the door to the coal shed was latched tight. Johnny was nowhere to be found.

"Darn that Mae Ella!" Willie Pearl was quick to blame her friend. "Thanks to you, Johnny got away."

Willie Pearl craned her neck down the road just in time to see Johnny disappear around the bend. And he was not alone. Four or five boys had joined him, kicking up stones as they went.

Willie Pearl quickly filled her bucket with rinse water. "If I hurry I can still catch him before he gets away." Willie Pearl rushed to complete her task. With a final swirl of suds, Willie Pearl was down the road, tracking behind her brother and his friends.

"There is one porch that holds fond memories for me, and that is the front porch of my mother's house in Jenkins, Kentucky. I wrote a chapter about that porch in my historical fiction book, Willie Pearl: Under the Mountain. I would be so pleased if you would include chapter two in your collection and I know my mom, Willie Pearl would be thrilled as well".

Michelle Y. Green

About the author
Michelle Y. Green is the daughter of Willie Pearl Mahone and Eddie Lee Young, of #5 and #6 hollers in Jenkins, Kentucky. A graduate of the University of Maryland with a B.S. in Journalism, Michelle, with her husband Oliver, is a principal of the Greentree Group, Inc. -- a writing/editorial/design firm in Temple Hills, Maryland. Their son, Brian is an avid reader and likes to create books of his own.

About Willie Pearl
Willie Pearl Mahone left the mountains of Kentucky in 1944 and married Eddie Lee Young, one of the first triple-rated black pilots in the Army Air-Corps. Pearl has traveled extensively, yet always finds time to travel to #6 to visit Jessie Mae, Susie Mae, and Johnny several times a year. Little brother Clint, now in Ohio, comes down often. Pearl lives in southern Maryland where she divides her time among her three daughters – Marie, Michelle and Adrienne – and three grandchildren – Shannon, Brian and Brandon.

"My earliest memories are of a back screened-in porch. I could not have been more than two or three at the time those memories formed, because we moved from the house with that porch when I was four. In these memories, I am standing on my mother's lap. She is seated in a rocking chair, a traditional wooden one with a high back. I could stand on her lap and hold onto the two knobs at either side of the top of the rocking chair and "ride" while she rocked.

We must have spent a lot of time out there together. I have memories of the view from that porch. I could see past the houses and up a hill on the left. There was a road along the crest of that hill that led to the shopping district. One day my sisters and their friends went to the movies but I was too young to go. I was on the porch with my mother when their little troop passed along that road as they walked to the movie. Perhaps the surprise of seeing them caused me to remember this.

Since I was so young my memories are only impressions with a few clear images. It was not some trauma that made me remember them, however. There is nothing frightening about them. They are very pleasant memories of security and time alone with my mother.

That is the only part of that house of my earliest childhood that I remember. I do not see my bedroom or the kitchen, just the porch. I have been fond of porches ever since. For me, a porch says home. There aren't enough good porches built on houses anymore."

Madeline Hunter
Pittsburgh, Pennsylvania

"For me, a porch says home."

About the Author:
Madeline Hunter has been celebrated as "one of the brightest new writers in the historical romance genre." (Publishers Weekly) Her first novel, By Arrangement, received the Waldenbooks Bestselling Debut Romance Author award. Her historical romances have garnered critical praise and numerous readers' poll awards, and have been USA Today bestsellers and Waldenbooks mass-market bestsellers. In the fall of 2003, Bantam released Madeline's Seducer trilogy back-to-back, over three months as part of its year-long 'Get Connected' promotion of historical romance. Madeline lives in Pennsylvania with her husband and two sons.

The following are the closing pages of the novel, **The Songcatcher** by Sharyn McCrumb.

Spencer smiled, "I hear you're looking for a song," he said.

"Well, I'll be damned, you know it?"

"Yeah. 'The Rowan on the Grave.' Used to play it on the guitar when I was in college. Nora Bonesteel came in today, and after one thing and another, she asked me what my grandmother's maiden name had been. This is not the sort of conversation I have with Miz Bonesteel, so I was mildly astonished, but I told her, 'Esther McCourry,' I said, 'married Spencer Arrowood, who I'm named after."

"And she said, 'I thought so.' And then she asked if I knew this song with the phrase, '. . . and when she's back home she will be changed' in it, and I said I did. Then she told me to find you and give you the words. 'Pass it on,' she said, as if it were the most important thing in the world."

"We're cousins," said Lark. "I didn't know that. And you have the song."

"Yes. I learned it when I was about twelve. They sang it at your grandmother's funeral."

"They did not!"

He smiled. "No I didn't mean at the church service. Afterward when the family went back to the house for a cold supper and to visit, all the men went out on the back porch, and one of them had a guitar, and they sang for a couple of hours. They sang that one twice."

Lark pictured the tiny screened-in porch on the back of the Walker's tidy box of a brick house. The men sat out there in the dark, with only the glow from lit cigarettes relieving the blackness. And they sang. But it was only the men. Girls of twelve were not allowed to tag along after the menfolk anymore. The charmed circle was closed. But Lark wanted to be where the music was. She crept out of the house and sat down on the steps outside the screened-in porch. Hidden by the storm door from the view of the guitar players, she listened until her mother called to make her go in. She could not remember seeing Spencer there at all. But she remembered hearing the song. It had resonated somehow. It was the family's ballad. It was her song.

"Sing it for me," she whispered.

And in the darkened back booth of Dent's Café, Spencer Arrowood sang.

About the author:

Sharon McCrumb, an award-winning Southern writer, is best known for her Appalachian 'Ballad' novels, set in the North Carolina and Tennessee mountains. The latest of these, Ghost Riders (Dutton 2003), is an account of the Civil War in the Appalachians and its echoes in the region today.

Ms. McCrumb's books have been translated into ten languages, and she was the first writer-in-residence at King College in Tennessee. In 2001 she served as fiction writer-in-residence at the WICE Conference in Paris.

Sharon McCrumb, a graduate of UNC, Chapel Hill with an MA from Virginia Tech, has lectured on her work at Oxford University, the Smithsonian Institution, the University of Bonn, Germany, and at universities and libraries throughout the country where her books are studied. She lives and writes in the Virginia Blue Ridge.

Just Being Frank

As told from the porch of Frank Raflo

If you drive about three miles north of Leesburg on Route 15, you will come to the intersection with White's Ferry Road. They are widening the intersection now so you can't miss it. Turn right and drive about a mile and you will come to the Potomac River and the White's Ferry crossing.

I know White's Ferry well. My dad kept a small boat out there and at least once a week we would go fishing. The fish did not bite well if you stayed close to the ferry, but if you went upstream to where Limestone Branch empties into the river, the fishing was good.

I haven't fished there in some time, but in the days when we did, the river had a lot of catfish, bass, eels, crappies and smooth-scale suckers. My mom ground up those suckers and made delicious fish cakes.

*Back row, left to right:
Frank Raflo; mother, Fanny;
father, Joe and brother, Harry
photographed in the field behind
their clothing store, Raflo's, on
King Street in Leesburg, Virginia.*

As a boy I liked to go to the river to swim, but my dad always insisted that he needed to "take a line along just to see if they are biting." He was a great one to get up at five in the morning and go out to White's Ferry to fish. He really believed that you could catch more fish at sunup than at any other time.

At this writing, the river is down about five feet, but the present operator of the ferry says it has never been shut down because of low tide.

I went to Thomas Balch library to see what I could find about White's Ferry. I found more than I had bargained for. It seems there has been a feature article about White's Ferry written about every twenty years. The ferry boat is known as the Jubal Early. In one of the articles I found the story of Jubal Early.

A portion of that article follows:

> *"Jubal Early, a West Pointer, lawyer and ex-Indian fighter from Franklin County, Virginia took the command of Stonewall Jackson's 13,000 troops after his death. While returning from his Washington raid, he crossed the river at White's Ford (a point below the ferry landing) on July 14th 1864. He was the only confederate to come within striking distance of the capitol.*
>
> *In fact, President Lincoln had a steamboat in the Potomac just in case he might need to evacuate. After his (Early's) defeat by Custer at Waynesboro in March, 1865, he was relieved of his command. He fled to Mexico and then to Canada in 1866. In 1869 he returned to Virginia to practice law and was with General Beuregard, a director of the Louisiana Lottery. He never took the oath of allegiance to the United States after the Civil War and was a rebel to the end. Today, our General Jubal A. Early remains as the only cable-guided (captive) ferry on the East Coast and the only ferry on the Potomac river.*

There was also a feature story about White's Ferry in the October 14, 1954 edition of *The Blue Ridge Herald*, a paper that was published in Purcellville for many years. A portion of the article follows:

> *" It's doubtful that White's Ferry, as an investment, will ever show any great profit. But as a symbol of the past, a little bit of history preserved for us, it*

is of incalculable value and makes all who hold these things dear want to say a warm 'thanks' to the men whose efforts have gone into it."

In December, 1982, Waterford historian Eugene Scheel did a lengthy history of White's Ferry, called, *Leesburg Reopens the Ferry*.

Scheel wrote that *". . . in the last decade of Colonial time there were six crossing of the Potomac within a 14 mile stretch of the river. One was Conrad's Ferry, today's White's Ferry"*. The article details all of the past owners and operators of the ferry. Scheel concluded his piece with the following paragraph:

"Otherwise, rather than the time honored saying that an owner of White's Ferry 'owns a piece of history', the ferry being the one survivor of its species across the Potomac, R. Edwin Brown prefers to phrase his share 'a quasi-eleemosynary operation,' and in case there is no big dictionary about, that phrase means, 'almost dependent on support from charity'."

Whether "charity" or business, today the ferry seems busier than ever.

About the Author: *Frank Raflo, referred to fondly by friends and associates as "Mr. Leesburg," has earned the admiration of many for his tireless efforts on behalf of the community. Frank served Leesburg as mayor, county supervisor and chairman of the Loudoun County Board of Supervisors. Now in his early eighties he remains active on the Governor's Council of Virginia Towns and writes his weekly column 'Just Being Frank,' for the <u>Leesburg Today</u> newspaper.*

Porches of Paris

That title is misleading. There are no porches in Paris. Well, known to compare with the great American porch. But we had *une terrasse*, eight stories up (Paris limit). The entire rooftop complete with wooden deck and railing which our landlord, *Monsieur Blue Eyes,* installed for our use alone. Oh, he could visit, *bien sûr*. It was glorious! A panorama of beautiful Paris in every direction, a view dominated by the Eiffel Tower *(le Tour E fell)*.

by L. Claire Kincannon

Near-by buildings are just a jump away — In a city that had a disastrous fire a couple hundred years ago, there are still no fire escapes, only ladder rungs — nice for escaping from burning buildings — nice also for *le voyeur* (my translation: rapist) who invaded my rooftop while Spouse was away in Mongolia. But I think I already told you that harrowing experience. And it was before our landlord installed the deck — before I lugged up huge clay pots and tons of dirt, 100s of geraniums and one tall wisteria plant which everyone predicted would not thrive on that windy porch in the sky. They were right. But I did. It was my inspiration — my daily dose of magnificent Paris reached by a narrow steep stairway, where I had all visitors autograph walls and ceiling, only to realize too late I would never be able to take the wall home with me to Paeonian Springs. Had to settle for photographs, which someday I'll enlarge and recreate on wallpaper. But for now let me take you back up the narrow steep stairway, surrounded by memories, to my porch in the sky.

No matter the time of day, it was always a treat. We'd have breakfast, brunch, dinner or just relax and read the paper shaded by a large green umbrella. At night, we could people-watch in the buildings *en face*, especially interesting if we, or I should say I, thought to bring up the binoculars. (Spouse never became *un voyeur*). I adapted.

One memorable event was an eclipse of the sun at the noon hour. We invited several couples to join us for a luncheon to watch this unique event. We wandered the rooftop wearing protective 3-D wrap-arounds like we wore to watch the movie, *Bwana Devil*, (remember that one?) and although it didn't get completely dark, the birds stopped singing — there was an eerie stillness in that twilight of an otherwise brilliant sunny day.

Bastille Day, or better, the eve of Bastille Day, 13th of July, was another memorable moment spent on our rooftop haven. All of the suburbs around Paris displayed their fireworks on the eve of the holiday. That meant from our perch we just had to swivel our heads in a grand circle and be treated to an"oohing-and-ahhhing" display, the likes of which I had never seen, unless it was the main show the next night which took place right above le Tour E fell, which meant it was practically above our heads.

And that brings me to the magical night at the changing of the millennium. We had the privilege of again hosting an event so momentous I get chills all over again when I think about it . . . 3 . . . 2 . . .1. . .WOW! *Le Tour Eiffel* explodes in a sea of sparkling colored lights. It's a new century. The spectacle will be forever etched in my brain. That will have to suffice since every New Year's Eve since then, I have watched 'the ball drop' on my 26" television screen while sitting alone (Spouse gone to bed. Does not like "forced fun") in my Paeonian Springs, Virginia living room. Somehow it's not the same. I do miss my Paris porch.

The author spent eight years in Paris and wrote <u>Paeonian to Paris</u> chronicling her humorous adventure coping with the French. Porches of Paris is an excerpt from her new book, <u>Paris to Paeonian with Fresh Eyes</u> due to be published in 2006 Dancingink Press.

Nancy Barnhart

Alice Beaton Malloy

Joe Davitt • Katherine Carter

Mary Bowman-Khrum • Regina Driscoll

Adrienne Marra • Del. Joe T. May

Lucille Boudreaux • Dianne Kinkead

Justin Owens • Edward Spar

John Devine & Bronwen Souders

Jane Elizabeth Brown Muncaster

Betty Stickler • Sen. Russell Potts

Jane Norman Scott

Porches Past

Kenny Barnhart July 1984

"Well, we certainly have enjoyed our porch, so this should be easy!

Probably the best thing about our big porch has been how much unique space it has added to our daily lives. On rainy days it was the perfect place for two lively little boys to build a play house out of porch rockers or carve pumpkins or race remote control cars. As those little boys got bigger, their porch antics grew with them. The wooden stairs became the perfect launch site for skateboards, sleds, and eventually snowboards. In the summer hardly a night has gone by where we don't spend an hour or two in the rockers talking, or better yet, listening. When the field in front of the house was planted in corn we really *could* just sit and hear the corn growing in the night.

One of our favorite moments on the porch was a night when we were rocking quietly listening to the night sounds. We heard a subtle but definite ruffling noise and looked down on the lawn where the moonlight revealed a pair of barn owls and four little owlets, maybe on their first excursion. We were lucky enough to watch for quite a while before they took off again.

The porch is like a hedge or fence row, allowing two worlds to merge, each leaving the other unspoiled. That makes it just about the most important room in the house."

Nancy Barnhart Purcellville, Virginia

"Growing up

on a farm near Unison, much time was spent on the front porch in the evenings and Sunday afternoons after church. I loved the hollyhocks; an array of colorful blooms, peeking over the banister. We spent time snapping beans, shelling peas, churning butter, sipping sassafras iced tea, and frequently talking with a neighbor who had 'just dropped by.' The movement of the old wicker swing gave us a respite from the smothering summer heat.

Memorable sunsets and rainbows were enjoyed and I assumed God made these just for us. They always made me smile."

Alice Beaton 'Benny' Malloy Unison, Virginia

One day when I was six years old, I was sitting on a porch swing with my sister and two cousins. It wasn't very nice outside. There was two feet of snow on the ground, so we were freezing. All four of us were playing around trying to see how high we could swing, so I, being a little daredevil, told everyone to watch because I could swing the highest. I started to swing and got higher and higher. The swing started to shake and I was wondering what could be wrong. My sister was shaking the swing trying to scare me so I would get off because she was mad that I was going high. The next thing I know I'm on the ground. I didn't know exactly what happened, but I knew I was in pain. I lifted my head and there was a big puddle of blood under me. My sister had been shaking the swing so violently I fell off and hit my chin hard on the cement porch floor. I started crying hysterically because I had never seen so much blood before in my life. My mom and aunt ran outside wondering what was going on. They both saw the puddle of blood and immediately took action. I was still lying there on the ground, so they picked me up and carried me in the house. They looked at my chin and decided I needed stitches and needed them quick. They called for an ambulance, but with two feet of snow on the ground there was no possible way an ambulance was going to make it down my aunts driveway. My aunt lives on a big horse farm so they decided when the ambulance got to the entrance of the drive, the owner and my uncle would be waiting with horses to transport the paramedics. I would need to get my stitches, up at the house. It took about an hour-and-a-half for the ambulance to finally get there. I was panicking because it was my first time ever getting stitches, but my family calmed me down. The paramedics rode up on horseback. By that time, I was pretty calm, until she brought out the needle. I didn't feel so sure of myself, then. But the lady paramedic was very nice to me and made sure I was going to be okay before she started stitching. Everyone got to watch me get my stitches, so I knew nothing bad was going to happen. It was not like being in a hospital room, all alone with nothing to look at. She finally got the job done and afterwards gave me some lollipops to make me feel better. My family still teases me to this day about making the paramedics ride horses to stitch my chin up with four little stitches. But I know now I will never swing high on another porch swing in the middle of winter.

Loudoun Valley High School student, Katherine Carter Purcellville, Virginia

the CIRCUS from my front porch

In Syracuse, New York, 1940, posters and billboards announced the most exciting part of the summer season: the arrival of Ringling Brothers & Barnum & Bailey Circus, "The Greatest Show on Earth."

Our front porch faced the street that led the three miles from the railroad depot to the 100-acre park where roustabouts would erect a colorful canvas city for one day.

Three trains filled with animals, acrobats, tents and wagons unloaded at the depot. About 5 am, the first train with the cook tent and brightly painted supply wagons began the three-mile trek. The following trains, in orderly chaos, unloaded and formed up for the procession to the park.

Our front porch was a grandstand seat for me and three other seven-year-old neighbors. We would cheer and clap as the wagons came by, some pulled by a team of horses and others as part of a three or four wagon train pulled by Mack trucks. Then came the animals. They didn't ride in trucks. They walked, as in a great parade. Young boys would run alongside, up and down the street announcing what was coming next. There were the horses and the zebras. Then, most excitedly the boys would yell: "Here come the elephants!"

In those days, Ringling Brothers touted fifty elephants. They came in two groups. First, the working elephants that were needed to pull canvas and unload the long tent poles. Later, the elephants that had paraded the night before in the grand finale in Rochester, now lumbered down to the Syracuse show grounds. One of the very young elephants walked near the curb and wrapped her trunk around a small-planted sapling and easily uprooted it to the cheers from our porch. The upset trainer administered a few quick blows and the playful elephant dropped the sapling.

By 11 am all the animals, wagons, and workers had arrived. The excitement for seven year olds was exhausting. After a little lunch, my mother would take us to the circus grounds where there was a world of wagons and tents – a city of canvas and cotton candy. Although we did not go into the Big Top, just looking around the circus grounds, I was sure this was certainly "The Greatest Show on Earth."

We returned home. From 7 pm until midnight the circus folded their tents, and headed to the waiting trains taking them to Utica for the next day's show. I spent some time on the porch watching the departing procession of wagons and horses. I was a little sad as I watched them silently pass by.

The next year I was eight going on nine. I had outgrown the porch. I was old enough to go to the circus grounds. I became part of the circus. Running water buckets to elephants and working as part of a gang pulling canvas. I was earning tickets to the Big Top. But in some ways, I missed watching the circus parade from our porch.

Joe Davitt Syracuse, New York

Our

Mary Bowman-Khrum with her father, Emory Bowman.

Note empty milk bottle, waiting for the milkman to pick up and deliver next morning. Note also the open mail box. Mail was delivered twice a day until about 1944.

With her mother, Evelyn Bowman.

house

and hundreds of Monopoly board look-alikes had quickly been thrown up outside the Aberdeen Proving Ground in Maryland. Families of soldiers suddenly drafted to serve their country moved in just as quickly. Like the house itself, the porch was tiny and poorly constructed. To my friend Dee—still my friend 60 years later—and me, it was more than a porch. We spread out our dolls and teddy bears to make it the floor of our beloved stuffed friends' open-air house. The words air conditioning, of course, had no meaning in the early 1940s, but the porch offered shade and sometimes a cooling breeze on hot summer days. We spent long afternoons with our stuffed toys and also read and played with paper dolls on the porch.

Some evenings the wail of sirens announced an alert and all lights had to be turned off. Thankfully for us, real planes did not drop bombs to devastate our lives, and I ate homemade lemon meringue pie or cookies by the light of the moon reflected on the tiny porch.

In those days materials went toward the war effort, not to frivolous appliances civilians didn't need. But one day, by a miracle, someone gave my father a new (probably black market) toaster. No more toast burned in the oven. This wondrous appliance of chrome and black stood on the table. Dee and I happily put a slice of bread in the trays on each side. My mother plugged the toaster's cord into the wall, and we watched the coils turn red. After a minute we opened the door on one side and, to our delight, the piece of bread flipped over. Door up and the coils browned the bread's other side. Amazing! My mother made Dee, her mother, and me hot chocolate. We sat on the porch and ate toast slathered with margarine, a wartime substitute for butter. Margarine was palatable only after my mother mixed the yellow food coloring that came in a little packet with the white block of grease. No matter! The toast and hot chocolate tasted great.

The house, with its porch, was eventually demolished. The dolls and teddy bears are in the past. The toaster is long gone. So too are the awful World War II spreads for bread. Only memories remain. And war.

Mary Bowman-Khrum is an author and professor at Johns Hopkins University.

moving here

in the summer before ninth grade, my family and I didn't know anyone. We relied on each other's company.

It was the hottest summer on record for Virginia in years, and we just couldn't keep the house cool enough. During that summer, my family and I sat out on our back porch all day. My mom would make an ice cold pitcher of tea and relax and talk about what was going on in our lives. Then, when the sun went down, my mother and father would get my brother all ready for bed and they would read him stories and rock him until he fell asleep. His favorite story was *The Night Before Christmas*; no matter what time of year it was. They would sit out on the porch for hours and hours, until they couldn't keep their eyes open any longer.

The best night was when we had a huge thunderstorm. We all sat outside on the porch, even Lily and Daisy, our two puppies. It was pouring down rain, and we were all getting soaked from the mist. But we didn't move. We didn't care. We loved it. Our greatest family memories were made on that porch.

Lucille Boudreaux Lovettsville, Virginia

We always referred to it as *The* Porch even though there were three porches on our house. It was called *The* Porch because many major activities occurred on that particular one: taffy pulling, feeding the dogs, visiting with friends, cooling off after fits of pique between brother and sister plus lots more, all took place there.

The Porch floor attracted numerous activities, but its roof was the focus of other attention. Colonies of mean-spirited and irritable hornets favored an intersection between the porch roof and the main house as a nesting place during the summer months. Woe to the human being who managed to become the object of attention of these winged hypodermic needles whose enthusiasm for attack was exceeded only by their ability to inflict pain.

One summer in my teen years, Mother asked me and my friend Turk (Turk because he received a scholarship in Poultry Husbandry to Virginia Tech presumably to learn about turkeys) to destroy a hornets nest at the junction of *The* Porch roof and the house. The strategy revolved around getting on to *The* Porch roof and spraying the hornets with insecticide while avoiding hostile hornets.

TURK vs HORNETS....

A small window opened onto *The* Porch roof from the room in which I slept. My task was to hold the window open while Turk climbed through and onto the roof. A Bug-Bomb, very popular then, would be squirted on the nest to eliminate any hornets in the nest and equally important, any hornets flying, which posed a threat to Turk.

All went well until a few very angry hornets began to fly up the spray column and approach Turk. Turk yelled, "Get the window open," and began a very hasty retreat to safety. He reckoned without thought of the slippery film of spray on the porch roof. One foot shot high in the air like an overachieving place-kicker, (which he was). He teetered near the edge of the roof a second or two and then recovered his balance, scrambling to safety, all the while yelling, "Get that window open!" Later, he told us, he felt like an airplane without enough altitude to pull out of the dive.

Delegate Joe T. May Leesburg, Virginia

My Uncle

stayed with us for several years while I was growing up. He helped us work our farm in the Shenandoah Valley near New Market and closely followed our farming efforts. Since we were at the mercy of weather, rain was a very welcome event for several reasons. It helped us ensure proper crop growth, and it gave us a very welcome break in operations particularly during the summer heat.

Whenever there was rain, or even the suggestion of rain, Uncle Earl and I would take two straight back chairs and move

Earl

onto the porch. There we watched the rain fall. And Uncle Earl listened intently. He claimed that he could hear the corn grow when it rained. We talked about a lot of things while we watched, because it was a setting which fostered reflection on life and things in general. Uncle Earl had a profound appreciation for hard work and honesty, and we seldom witnessed a rainfall without commenting on the absolute value of both of these human attributes. But we talked about many things ranging from his experience during World War II to my tractor driving skills (he felt I was a little reckless) to the fortunes of our various neighbors, and how they got there along with dozens of other topics.

The basic objective of these porch sessions was recreation for Uncle Earl and me, but the philosophy, wisdom, and human values eventually transferred were far more valuable than the simple human amusement.

The porch remains, but Uncle Earl is gone. I visit there occasionally, and my mind bridges fifty-five years and I still recall those porch conversations . . . .

Delegate Joe T. May

"In my day,

mid 1950s, kids had to play outdoors. You were outside from early in the morning until late at night. Oh yes, you could come in to use the bathroom (not too often) and maybe eat a meal, but you played outside. No exceptions!

My house had an L-shaped porch leading to the front door of the house and ending with stairs to the backyard. The porch is where my big brother and I played during every season. We played cowboys and Indians. We played cops and robbers. We tried out our roller skates and played hockey. I can still see my brother and his friends with their stamp collecting albums sitting around a table sorting their stamps. When it was snowy and freezing cold, we bundled up, ran around to keep warm and played together on the porch. Many picnics were eaten there and on warm summer nights we were allowed to camp out. The night sounds might have been scary, but at least we were almost in the house which was a comfort.

As all little girls do, I grew up and moved away. Whenever I return 'home,' I make it a point to drive by my old house. There it stands, a little older, but still the same. I wonder if other kids play out on the porch."

Dianne Kinkead Great Falls, Virginia

"The fondest memory I have of my porch

is going to retrieve super long home runs that I or someone else had belted during a friendly, yet competitive game of wiffleball. These games would take place during the summer when my friends would drive to my house, and we would spend all day playing home-run-derby or just a regular five-inning game. The game would get fierce and intense, so intense, that my friends would hurl the bat, or rock, into oblivion when they struck out. Then there would be bad calls one way or another. This would lead to base-tossing, name calling, and dirt kicking. I would then silence the crowd with a swing of my bat, sending the ball over the fence and altogether cracking the ball in half (this ball cracking never really happened, but you can imagine the reaction from my cronies if it did happen). Jesus himself would congratulate me for the wonderful display of heroism and sportsmanship. My friends would get honorable mention. Of course, these tales are fantastic, but I am telling you, I am a force to be reckoned with on the wiffleball field. No matter what, there would be titanic home runs that would not just land on the deck, but bounce off windows, shingles, and airplanes. The day would then end with a tall glass of Kool-Aid.

Justin Owens Lovettsville, Virginia
student at Loudoun Valley High School

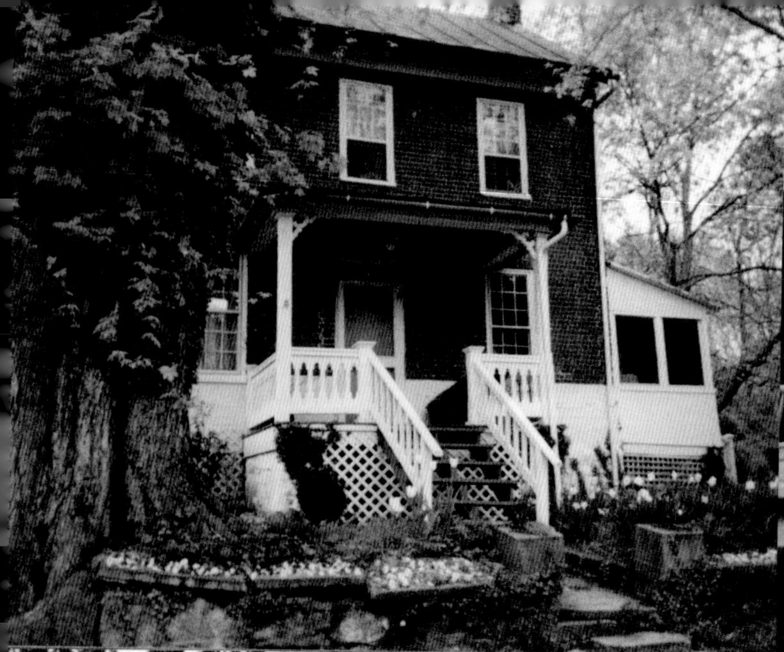

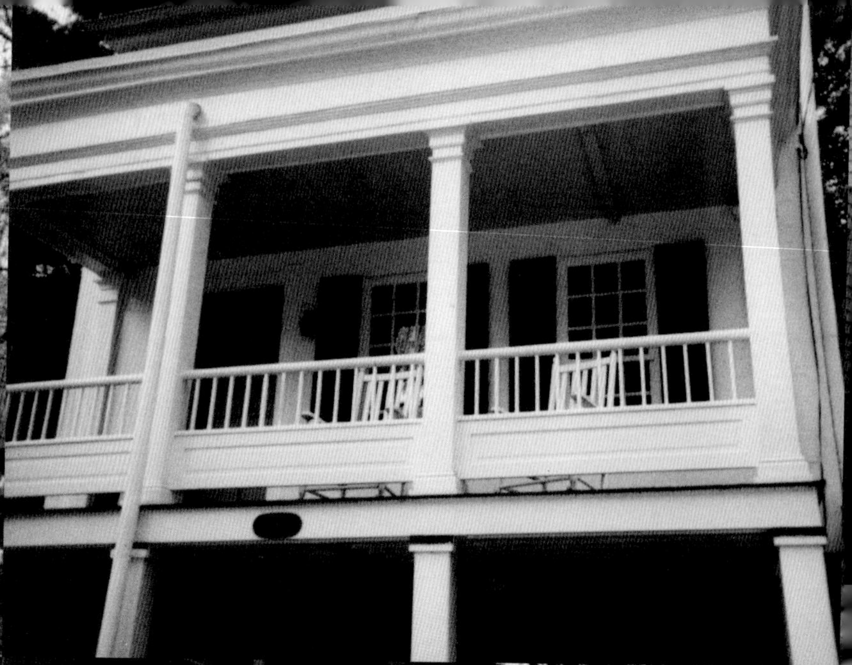

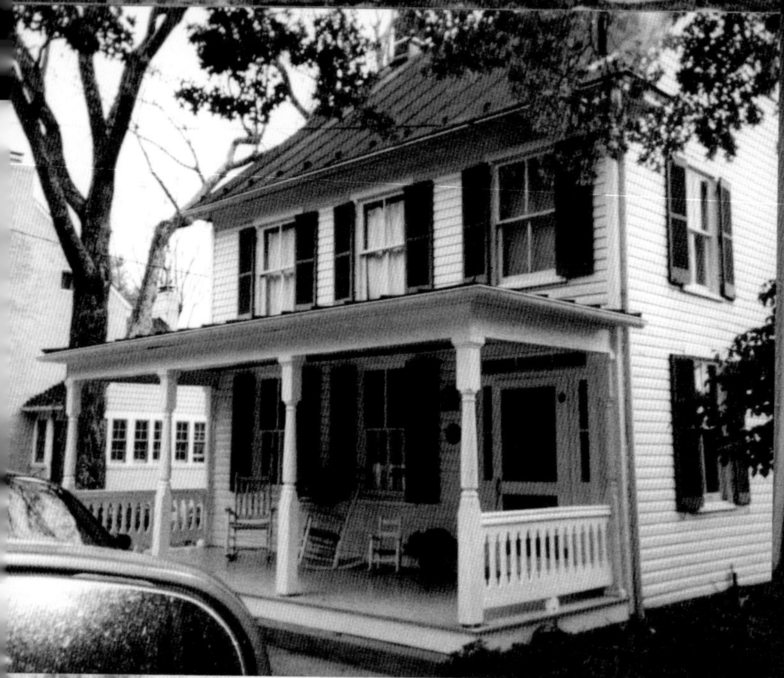

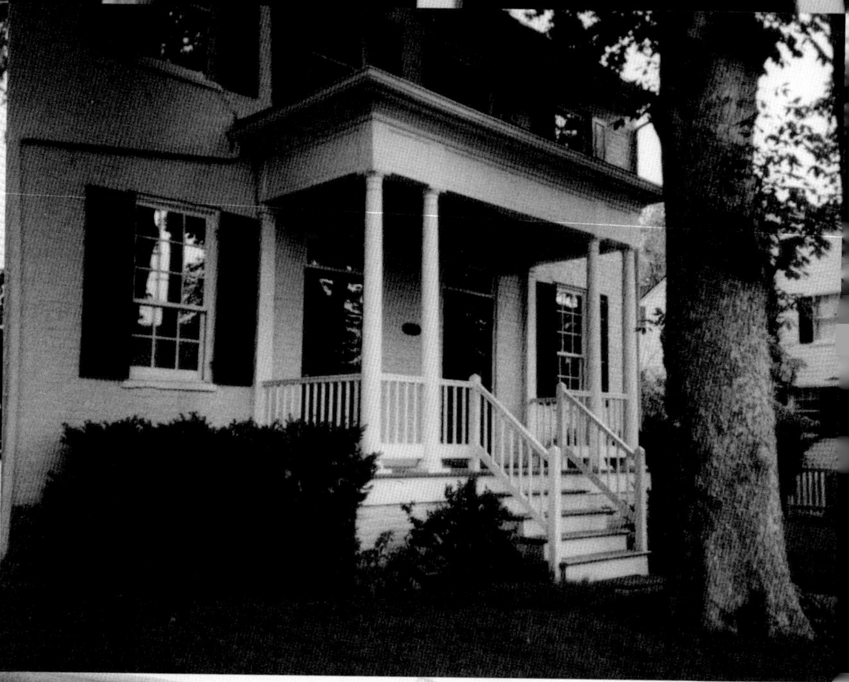

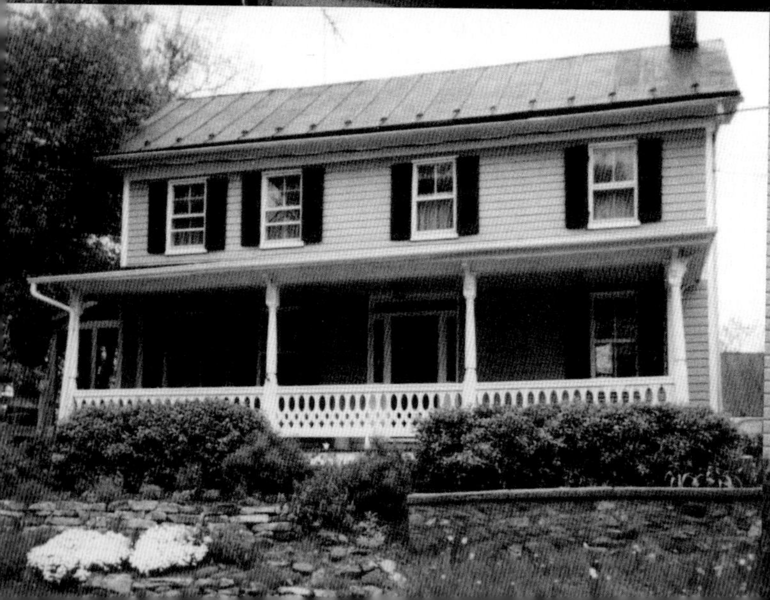

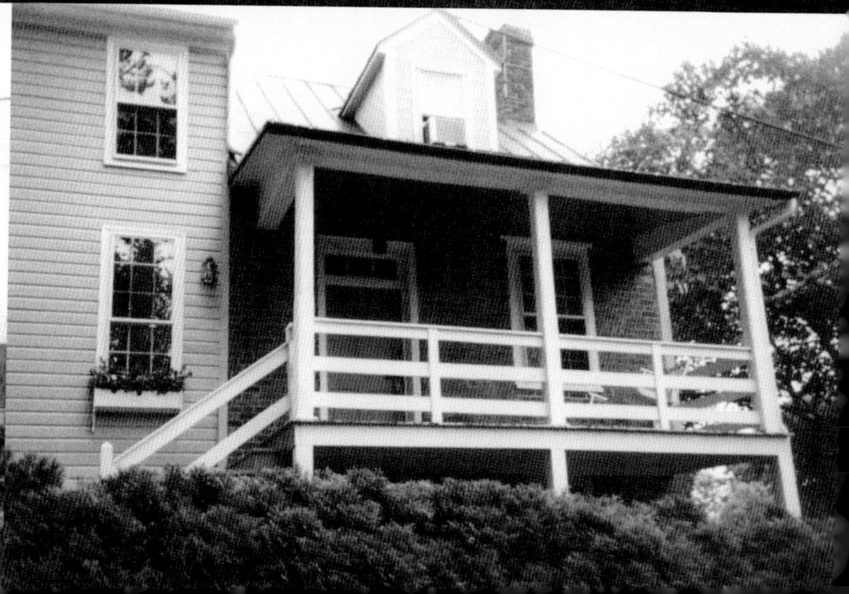

Porches of Waterford

By John Divine *annotated by Bronwen Souders*

For some years walking tour guides had cavalierly described the porches of Second Street, at least, as having resulted from "a porch salesman who came through town in the early 1900s and sold a lot of people on porches." To our chagrin, we learned that the builder was, in fact, no salesman but John Divine's father, an eminently local 5th generation Waterfordian, and fine carpenter. It seemed therefore logical to ask John Divine to "say a few words" about porches. Neophyte historian that I then was, I assumed he would simply stand up and reel off a few stories from his childhood. But this was John Divine. He told me he spent a very pleasant afternoon driving up and down Waterford's few streets really thinking about the porches and meshing it with his lifelong love of the history of the town. Born in the village in 1911, John never lost his passion for the why and how and who of Waterford. He died in November 1996.

April 22, 1996: "There is the well-worn story of the visitor who asked the native of a small town what they did for excitement and/or entertainment. The reply was: "We go down to the barber shop on Saturday nights and watch a few hair cuts." I now know what the citizens of Waterford do on a Sunday afternoon for entertainment. They go to the Old School and listen to an uninformed person talk about porches. I am not certain that my remarks will be as entertaining as watching haircuts, but since Waterford does not have a barber shop, you have no other recourse but to listen to me.

I grew up with the Waterford porches and never knew until this past week how many different styles or kinds of porches existed, and how they had changed when I thought back to the days of my youth. Also, to play a word game or an ownership game, I will use the names in many cases of the owners at that time as I remember them.

The period of time covered is the 1920s and 30s. That is the time-frame that a porch of every design would show all over town. High porches, low porches, double porches, street level, front porches, side porches, back porches and wrap-arounds. You name it, we had it.

The question is often asked, "Why was the town located on this spot" where sloping hills fall away into meadows along creek banks. The answer might be Ball's Run and South Fork of Catoctin Creek, that is – water power – water power, a perfect channel for these two streams to flow through. A mill was started and the rest is history. Just like Topsy, it just grew. The early mill and the Quakers meeting house became a small trade center.

I mention the terrain for it was a contributing cause to the many types of porches that I will call to your attention. Certain locations dictated a certain house for that lot and consequently the accompanying porch.

Along the north side of Main Street where the houses are pushed back into the hillside, we find the double porch or second story porch. Here in my time the street level or first story was used on rare occasions for commercial purposes, but also for storage, principally fuel.

Now let's go for a walk . . .
The Cost House, or earlier Ratcliff House was a school.

The Potted Pear was O.H. Davis's Cash Grocery. Then we see Clarice Hough, Kitty Leggett, and George Dean as storage, Collins and Coats without porches. Then came CW Divine, living on the first floor; next came the tavern which I believe was on the street level. In my time, it was storage for the telephone office above, but with meat hooks around the walls. The telephone office and living quarters caused a split or two level porch, one for entrance to the living section and a lower level for entrance to the telephone office. The Arch House had a porch in the rear for living entrance, and on the street only steps into the store that occupied the street level. The next house had a side porch as its foundation. The first floor came to the edge of the street as this had originally been an iron storage house for a local merchant. Before I am reminded, this was not in my time, I only missed it by a century and a few years. The Pink House had a wrap-around second story porch and the street level was commercial.

On the north side of Main Street then, you can see what I mean by terrain dictating the type of porch. To further my assertion, let's look at the houses on the north and south sides of Main Street.

While the north side houses are pushed back into the hillside, those on the south side are built at the street line as there was not much room for setback – the land was inclined to be wet on that side. North side basements were relatively dry, those across the street were often too wet.

The Bank House porch on the south side consisted of a long concrete slab a few inches high, covered by a roof about eight feet above it. This property belonged to John Willy Kinney Sally Jones's house, one house up. It was built so near the street that a front porch was impossible. Instead, it had a frame side porch, as did Aunt Laura Page's next door.

The next four houses on the south side were without porches as their openings were one step down to the street. Further on, the present telephone office, which belonged then to 'Doc' White, a local vet, had a porch level with the street. The Graham House next to him, never had a porch street side.

Second Street, or 'New Town,' makes an interesting study in variety. The Spence Virts House had a narrow uncovered porch about three feet deep across the front, just wide enough for a rocking chair. The Spratt House had a covered porch across the front. Then there were several wrap-arounds: The Phillips/Carr House, Van Devanter, L.P. Smith and W.C. James. The Dr. Heaton House has a covered entrance, or as I termed it, a stoop. "Catoctin Creek"— the house, not the stream — had a cover over the slab at street level. The Charles Merchant House with a conventional front porch as did several more along Second Street: ie, Rickard, Moore, James and Hall Houses. The Parker-Bennett had a covered porch, I believe, in two sections as it was a double house. The Mansfield House was another wraparound, as was the William Williams place."

John's prepared text ended here. He went on to relate a story from his youth when a man was painting the porch at the William Williams House, and had a jar marked varnish. Even though the job involved painting, he seemed to fool everyone about the need for the 'varnish,' but he let John in on a secret: it was part of his afternoon pick-me-up.

John also recalled how long it could take neighbors from the far ends of town to get their mail and get back home, with all the non-mail-gathering neighbors sitting on their porches, chores done, and chatting with the strollers. Those porches had at least one final use. One descendant divulged that as a young girl, when the porch on her house was being built, she wrote a blushingly honest account of her crush on one of the boys in town and hid it in a pillar. Lest anyone start 'repairing porches,' that porch has already been removed.

The ~~Porch~~ Stoop at 176

To be exact, it was 176 Beach 70th Street, Arverne, New York. My house was about seventy-five yards from the Atlantic Ocean. Arverne, part of the Rockaway Peninsula, was deserted ten months of the year. In July and August during the Depression and WWII years, it was the temporary home of mostly Jewish families escaping the deadly heat of the Bronx and Brooklyn. It was a time to enjoy some of the softest sand on the east coast, and tame waters due to long jetties jutting out from the beach. Mothers stayed the whole summer with the kids, and fathers came out for the weekend on the Long Island Railroad from Manhattan. Bungalow colony rooms and converted mansions housed families of four, five and six in spaces that must have reminded them of their immigrant parents' cold-water flats on Hester, Broome or Delancy Streets in Lower Manhattan. Anyone visiting today will find deserted tracts of land where 176, a two family detached house once stood, torn down along with all the other houses on the street to build a huge housing development that never received the needed funding.

The area was New York's less expansive answer to the Catskills Mountains resorts. But that era of the 1930s, 40s and early 50s, came to a sad end with the demolishment of the permanent and summer housing . OK, so what does this have to do with a porch? Just giving you some flavor of the times and the place. From 1941 until 1952, I lived year 'round at 176, my parents renting from the Brills downstairs. The entrance to our upstairs apartment was accessed through two doors; one solid, and one glass-paned door facing the front of the house. To get to the door one first climbed the 'stoop,' our word for porch. Indeed, according to Webster, a stoop is "any small porch at the entrance of a house." We never called it a porch, way too high-fallutin' for working class families.

My most dramatic remembrance of our stoop was the then famous fly-over from Idyllwild Airport on the part of Army Air Force fighters and bombers on or about August 26, 1945. This was in celebration of our victory over the Japanese, the war ending on August 13th. My minds eye still remembers sitting there and watching what seemed like thousands of airplanes darkening the sky and the feeling of complete security in the knowledge that we were so powerful. That was also the summer the families on our street installed blackout shades that were required lest the Germans or Japanese figured out some way of bombing us. It was also the end of the patrols of soldiers on the boardwalk that ran for about four miles along the beach. At last we could buy ices and play games at the arcade on the boardwalk for which my mother gave me one dime a week. Given that games were either a penny or at the most two cents apiece you cannot imagine how long that dime lasted. And if you were hard working, which meant collecting the empty bottles on the beach and returning them to a candy store for two cents each, you might even win a prize from the automatic Gypsy lady machine that told your fortune, and randomly every now and then, dispensed some trinket that would be lost somewhere on the beach the same day.

Of course with the Cold War, our feelings of euphoria didn't last long, but that's another story. My parents, the owners from downstairs, whose apartment I never once went into, and the owners son, daughter-in-law and child who lived in the basement apartment, placed their beach chairs on the landing at the top of the stoop, and the kids sat on the steps. Indeed, a typical Sunday afternoon event was listening to the music fest. This consisted of stringing a wire from our upstairs three room apartment to a bakelite radio placed on the stoop so the old folks could listen to the Yiddish station, WEVD. To this day I remember my parents and those from downstairs laughing while listening to 'Joe and Paul' ads and Yiddish references to the mythical radio station WBVD (BVD, get it?). And for a bit of trivia, EVD stood for Eugene V. Debbs. One guess where the sentiments of the original Lower East Side immigrants in New York City stood.

As mentioned, the son lived in the basement with his wife and four year old. And much to my good luck, they had the first TV in the neighborhood. For all of you used to plasma TV's and the like, allow me to digress to the world of a twelve inch, black and white, tubed, rabbit-eared model made by Dumont. The year was 1948 and two significant TV shows entered my life. The first, thanks to the benevolence of the basement couple and their little one, was Howdy Doody. This show was the only event that could keep me away from the stoop. The second show, at eight o'clock on Tuesdays was the Texaco Star Theater with the one and only Milton Berle, aka "Uncle Miltie." With great fanfare, the four of us in my family, the two Brill's downstairs, and the basement family of three somehow scrunched into a living room built for two and roared with laughter over Uncle Miltie's antics.

So, back to the stoop. Indeed, our stoop eventually became, for me, an important venue as the site of one of the most important sports of those days – stoopball. First the ball. This was a regulation Spaulding, pronounced Spauldeen, for reasons that must be truly mythic. For some reason, we never got the hang of pronouncing the 'g.' When my wife reminds me of the fact that I still mispronounce Spaulding, I absolutely refuse to acknowledge such a fact. It would destroy wonderful memories.

Now to the game. Hitting the edge of a step and catching the ball was worth ten points. Five points if you only hit the inner step (a diagram here might help). Obviously, if you did not catch the ball you not only received no points, but were 'out,' and the ball passed to the next player. You only got one turn, and what you got was your score. You might think that a player could keep playing for hours, but in reality, you were expected to hit that stoop as hard as you could everytime. Trust me, your time 'at stoop' was never that long. Oh yes, I forgot. If you hit a fly ball and caught it, that was an extra ten points.

As mentioned, hitting the stoop hard was part of the game. That was easy. Hitting the stoop accurately was another matter. Let me explain. This was an old house, with an equally old stoop. Our landlord, though decent people (based on the minor number of complaints emanating from my parents), never really grasped the concept of upkeep. Hence the stoop had what I guess were to adults, minor flaws. But to those dedicated to attaining scores that would impress Joe DiMaggio, such cracks and chips that did exist were excessive. Of course at the same time these flaws added to the excitement and challenge of the game. Catching a ball that bounced in an unexpected direction due to hitting a cracked brick was macho in the extreme – although it didn't add to your point score. That was the good news. Ah, but on the down side, balls hitting these cracks were also liable to go in directions not intended by yours truly and those daring enough to challenge me. I must point out that I spent countless hours at this game, and considered myself a worthy champion of any imaginary World Series of Stoopball. I digress. When the Spauldeen hit a crack, it was just as likely to go in a direction opposite to that intended, namely backwards up the stoop. Of course this meant you were out, as there was nothing to catch. Worse, you were about to glean the wrath of both your parents and the landlord. The door at the top of the stoop had, as previously mentioned, a glass front, and to the right of the door was one of the front windows of the Brill's apartment. I know it may be hard to believe, but that Spauldeen could do serious damage to any window that got in its way – and it did. It went right though the pane, spewing glass all over the porch. Now what to do? Mrs. Brill, not hearing that well, and Mom, somewhere upstairs, did not hear the concussion. And me, standing there knowing that I was now about to be admonished, and with no way out, went off to our apartment. Up the stairs I went, with my 10-year-old forlorn look and sidled up to Mom and for the tenth, twentieth, God knows how many times, said, "Mom, guess what? We were playing stoopball, and . . . ." Nothing more needed to be said. With a look of annoyance, Mom responded with the expected, "Do you think money grows on trees?" "No Mom, I'm sorry," I replied contritely. Off Mom went to Mrs. Brill who shook her head in that way that only the old folks could, sorry for the fact that we had to pay for a new pane, but saying, "What can you do with these kids?" And to be honest, that was that. In other words, the wrath was both short lived and very mild. Maybe life and people were just nicer then, but the most I can remember of any other admonishments were statement such as, "you have to be more careful," and, with the best of Yiddish accents "oy vay." I did get to know the glazier though, and even challenged him to stoopball. For reasons that at the time I didn't understand, he never took me up on it.

Edward Spar Alexandria, Virginia

Locust &

Hamilton, Virginia

from *Old Stone Houses of Loudoun County, Virginia* by Salonge Strong

The trim stone house which sits on the south fork of Catoctin Creek about one mile outside Hamilton, Virginia near the Milling Company wears its great age with spirit. It's another of Loudoun County Virginia houses which has been built, owned and occupied by the same family throughout its entire history.

Though the datestone beneath the chimney of the wing reads 1837, the main section of the house is considerably older, probably dating as far back as 1785. Like others of its kind, it had originally a log wing which stood on the site of the present stone one.

Locust Grove's 634 acre tract was one of three transferred by Lord Fairfax to the English Quaker from Bucks County, Pa., Richard Brown, in 1741. Of the three, only Hunting Hill, near Taylorstown is no longer a Brown possession, its land being transferred very early to Thomas Taylor.

Locust Grove, however, passed from Richard Brown through one of his sons eventually to the late Miss Sarah Elma Brown who willed it to the present occupant. Like Oakland Green, it gives every evidence of carrying on its unbroken tradition.

rove

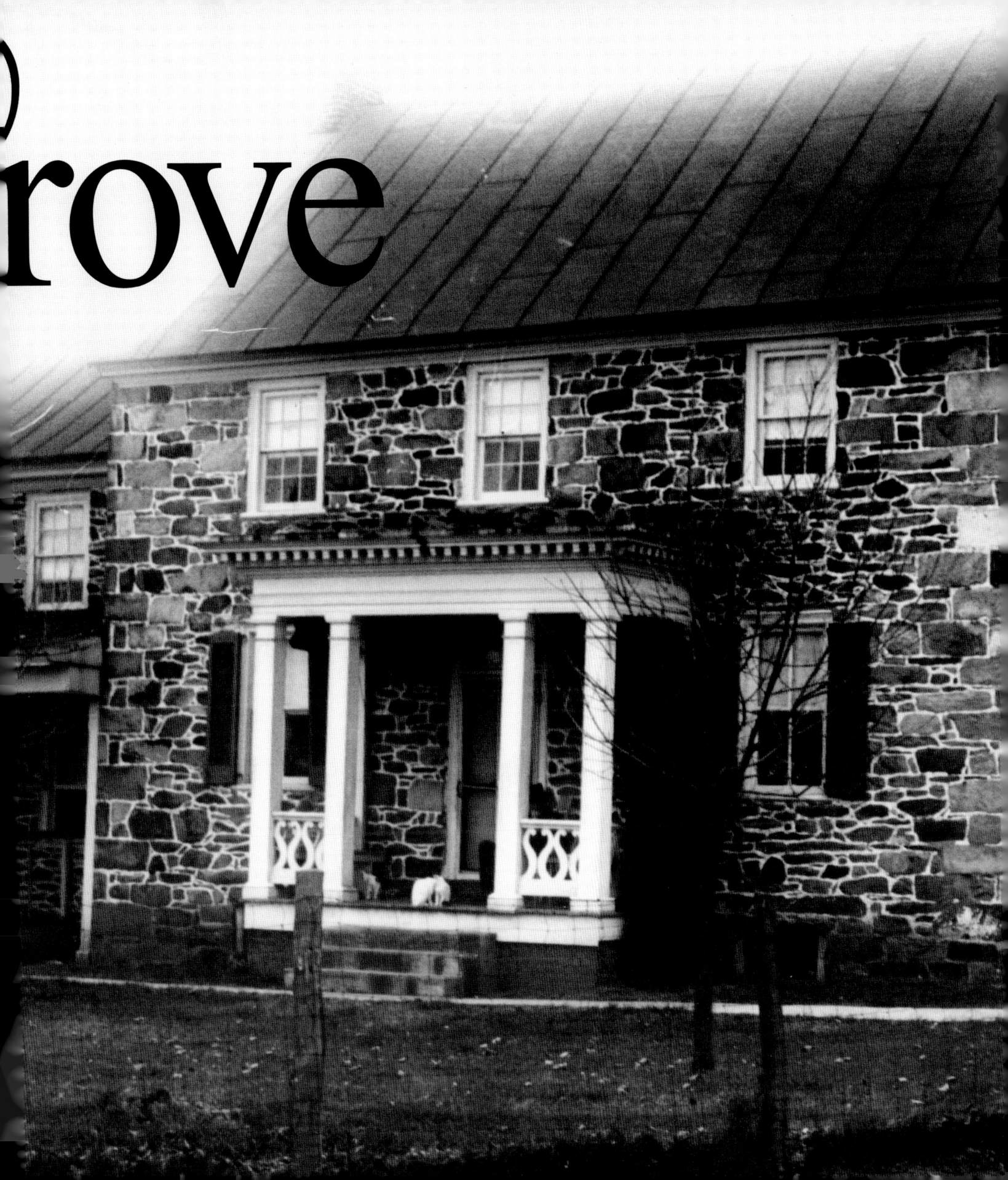

My Porch at Locust Grove

As a child the porch was one of my favorite places. I could play on the porch with my three brothers: Richard, Jr., Mason, and Joe. We played games, we chased each other back and forth, played tag — hide and seek. You could play on the porch spring, summer and fall. It kept you cool when it was hot and sheltered you when it rained or snowed. I remember as a child I would ride my little tricycle around and around and back and forth on the porch. Also, back then, relatives and friends visited all the time. There was nothing else to do after chores, so all your cousins, aunts and uncles came to visit and you'd sit on the porch catching up with each others lives. And then you would have a cookout or family picnic on that porch. The best time was making ice cream, taking turns cranking — making banana, peach, chocolate or vanilla ice cream. That was so good. Mom pulled my first tooth on the porch, and my brother's teeth too. When it got cold the only heat in the house came from burning wood, so my brothers and I kept one side of the porch filled with wood so it would stay dry to burn better. Then there was canning time. We'd sit on the porch snapping beans, shelling corn and shucking corn for mom to can.

Jane Elizabeth Brown on the steps at Locust Grove.

Jane Elizabeth Brown with her mother, Sarah Brown.

On the porch at Locust Grove.

Other fond memories from our life on the porch:

My mom singing to us while dad was plowing and waiting for him to come to supper; catching lightning bugs and putting them in a jar to see how much light they would give out in the darkness; sitting on the porch and taking pictures of all our cousins, aunts and uncles and friends when they came to the country 'to get fresh air'; just listening to the sounds of the birds or watching rabbits and squirrels play. As the young quiet days have now passed, I can still sit on my porch and remember those fond memories of family—family pets and things and moments spent on this, my old porch.

Jane Elizabeth Brown Muncaster
Locust Grove, Hamilton, Virginia
Grand-grand niece of William Henry Brown (on cover)

My Front Porch Story

Dedicated to Mabel Lee Carter Davis and Henry Davis

The porch was a place for quality family time. We would all share about our days and what went on. Occasionally, we would eat out on the porch or drink lemonade. Checkers and Dominos were our favorites to play outside during the warmer months.

The front porch on my grandparent's house in Greensboro, North Carolina was a wonderful place, too. My grandfather had crippling arthritis. He had to use crutches or, on a very good day, a cane. After breakfast, he would come out onto the porch and sit in an old green metal porch chair. He always greeted any, and all, of the people walking by.

He never knew a stranger. The house was on a steep hill and people huffed and puffed up the hill. My grandfather would ask people to come up on the porch and rest. We usually had lemonade or sweet iced tea ready for them. The visitors sat on the wonderful green metal glider and talked and talked.

We would also play my grandfather's favorite card game, Canasta. There was only one hard and fast rule about Canasta – and it was my grandmother's rule, "No cards on Sunday, especially not on the front porch."

I was in the first grade when I lived with my grandparents and played on the front porch. There was another little girl, just my age, who lived across the street. She would come over and we would play dolls or dress up on the porch.

My grandmother often let us water the many plants filling the porch boxes all around the edge. Geraniums, begonias, coleus and other beautiful plants made the porch a colorful spot. There was a big wooden barrel under the rainspout to gather the soft water for the plants.

That special porch was a place of love, support, fun and imagination for me. It was my grandfather's way to visit with the rest of world when he could no longer get around. It was my way to learn from his kindness and the blessing friendship can be to our lives. When my grandfather died, the church was filled with strangers, but not strangers to him. They were the people he had met on that wonderful front porch.

Betty-Lee Stickler, storyteller and teacher at Loudoun Valley High School, Purcellville, Virginia

"When I was a youngster,

I used to sit on the front porch of our old ramshackled apartment house and listen to my dad and Grandfather Potts swap stories.

I was particularly captivated by the fire engine stories. My grandfather used to tell me of the old Sarah Zane Fire Department and the horse drawn fire engines that would race to put out the fires.

My ambition in those days of youth was to be a fireman, so obviously, I was fascinated by the stories of the beautiful white horses that pulled the fire engine, and the stories of how the whole community would come out in force to help put out a blaze.

Every time I visit one of today's firehouses I think of those stories that my grandfather and dad used to tell me about the good old days and the horse drawn fire engines."

Senator Russell Potts Winchester, Virginia.

My porch memory

"At my grandparent's house along the river, they had a deck and gazebo overlooking the river lined with trees. I remember spending many summers lying out in the warm sun with my mom, grandma, and aunts.

We would sit out there and watch my grandpa and all the boys crabbing out in the boat, and then they would return and cook them up so perfectly! The entire family would help set the table with newspapers, knockers, and paper towels, and we would all get seated around the picnic table and pig out on the deliciously seasoned crabs!

During these summers I remember all the men of the family working hard building the porch, sweating in the hot sun, and then my mom would fix up some ice-cold lemonade and my sister and I would serve it to the boys hard-at-work.

So many great memories and family moments happened on the porch that my grandpa built with his own hands. They are irreplaceable!"

Regina Driscoll Lovettsville, Virginia

grew up in a quiet suburb called Pelham Manor, just outside of New York City, and although our home did not have a porch it did have a stoop. A stoop, for those who are unfamiliar with the term, is a small area of concrete extending from the front door with steps leading down to a sidewalk. My home was a Tudor-style brownstone with a fairly large stoop for sitting. Two chairs were always available. My memories are of many lazy days chatting with my mom, my friends and any nearby neighbors while enjoying the beauty of our tree-lined street. It was a peaceful and quiet neighborhood, and since the houses were attached on one side, a duplex, one could easily chat with a neighbor and not be obnoxious with "yelling" your conversation.

I now think back fondly, because in all the houses where I've lived since moving out shortly after college, I never did have another stoop or porch. Yes, I have had decks, patios both brick and slate, and even an enclosed sunroom, but I now know that it is not the same. Our stoop was the area of our home to relax and take a break, enjoy the fresh air on a nice day, and most often, the place to sit in the company of family members, friends and neighbors while watching the world go by.

I recall with fondness those memories of growing up in my childhood home during twenty-five years of my life, and my times-on-the-stoop memories are an integral part.

Adrienne Marra Sterling, Virginia

Childhood Memories of the front porch at Longmoor

Jane Norman Scott
Culpeper, Virginia

- Havng a tea party on my little table and chairs.

- Pushing my doll carriage up and down the porch.

- Learning to sew at my grandmother's knee.

- Family gatherings after supper in the cool of the evening as the cows grazed in the meadow at the foot of the hill.

- Porch columns serving as home base for Hide and Seek and Kick-the-Can.

- Family pictures taken here.

Jane Warren Norman with step-grandmother, Nonie Cary Dickerson and Uncle Joseph Coleman Dickerson, both visiting from Richmond.

Jane Warren Norman with mother, Isabel Dickerson Norman.

↪ Jumping over the boxwood and
　　running to the bottom of the hill

Longmoor

is built on part of the land granted to Sir Francis Awbrey by letters patterned from the proprietor of the Northern Neck of Virginia, dated July 7, 1731. This was a very large tract of land.

In 1732 Sir Francis Awbrey deeded it to Colonel John Tayloe as of record in Prince William County. On March 14, 1793, Colonel Tayloe and his wife, Ann, of Richmond County, Commonwealth of Virginia, sold it to James McIhany of Loudoun for 6,500 pounds, money of Virginia. James McIhany lived on this tract of land and his home became known as Ithica.

His daughter, Rosannah married Lewis Elsey who was a lawyer, taught school, was highly educated and served in the war of 1812. A two room school was built on this plantation near Longmoor, in which Lewis Elsey taught. It is said that it was built with stones that were left from building Longmoor.

The administrators of the estate of James McIhany were members of his family, Dr. John McIhany and Margaret McIhany, February 1814.

This property continued in the family. Rosannah Elzey deeded it to her daughter, Ann Elizabeth Elzey Washington and Ann's husband, Edward Sanford Washington. Ann Elzey and Edward Washington were married at Longmoor on April 14, 1829. They lived there where Edward farmed the land and raised livestock. Then a deed of Fayette Kentucky, indicated that the Washingtons had moved to Kentucky, for on May 29, 1829 it was recorded that they deeded Longmoor to Mary Cecilia Elzey White, a sister of Ann Elizabeth Elzey Washington, and Mary's husband, John R. White. The next deed passed the land to Robert J. T. White, presumably Ann Elzey's son.

In 1893 this property passes from the decendants of James McIhnay when Robert. J.T. White sold it to Fielder Norman. In 1943 the ownership passed to Edward Cole Norman who bought it from his father's estate, that of W. Fielder Norman. And it stayed in the Norman family until the year 2000.

From Loudoun Heritage by Evelyn Taylor Adams

March 16, 1941–third birthday party for Jane Warren Norman. Left to right: Betty Jane Hall, Aubrey Hall, Jr., (father founded Hall's Funeral Home in Purcellville), Dorothy Ann Hansbarger, Jane Warren Norman, Adele Hawthorne, Jean Anderson Farmer, Sandra Anderson, Manley Pancoast, David Tribby, Lynn Adams, Sandra Larrick.

Porches *in* Poetry & Painting

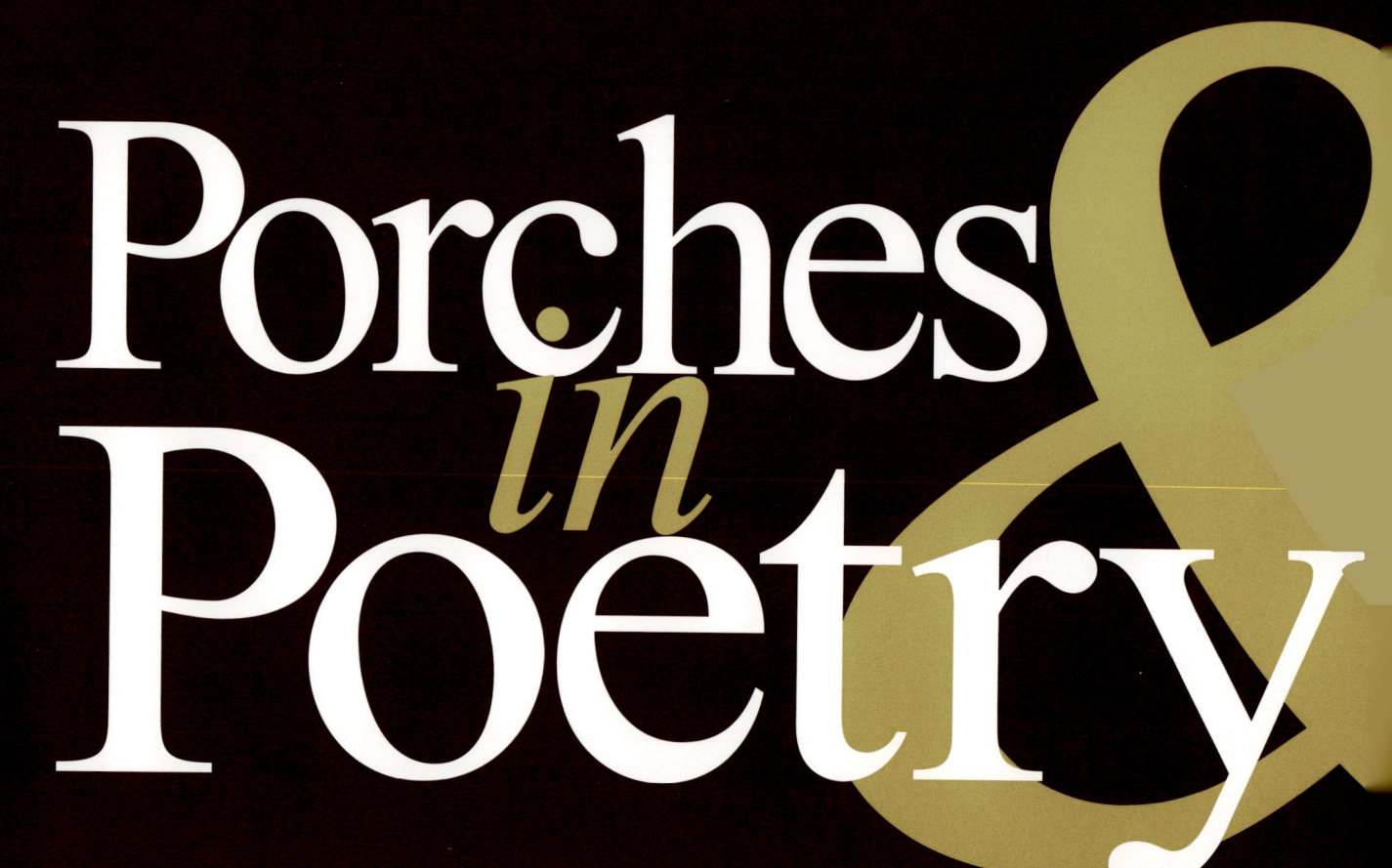

Jessica Williamson • Mason Balazs • Antonia Walker

Antonia Walker, Sunday Dinner 20 x 24 Oil on canvas

Lucille Dowell • Adriana Trigiani • Shirley Amos

All through my childhood in a town on the Mississippi River, my family would gather on porches of various relatives where there were always lots of rocking chairs and usually a hanging swing. But it was not until I moved to the Shenandoah Valley, after living in cities, that I noticed the magical quality of porches and began to include them in my work as a place where life happened, unfolding at a slower pace than when inside the house. It was then that I recalled the memories of my childhood, and tried to convey the quiet hot afternoons and long summer evenings with color and light.

Antonia Walker Waterford, Virginia

Antonia Walker, Grandparent's Porch 16 x 20 Oil on canvas

A Place

by Mason Charles Balazs
Student, Loudoun Valley High School

A place to sit,

A place to talk

A place to rest

A place to dream.

A place to watch the sun come up

A place to watch it go down

A place where time has no hold,

A place where I'd like to grow old.

A place where people come and go

A place that is always welcoming

A place with many names

My favorite place . . . my porch

Antonia Walker, Back Porch 16 x 20 Oil on canvas

Antonia Walker, Carpenter's Lace 30 x40 Oil on canvas

The Porch

by Shirley Amos
Purcellville, Virginia

*The porch can be a magical place. One can
look out over an endless space*

*With each changing season a different mural comes alive
In Summer, watch the hummingbirds drawing nectar
as they flutter and dive*

*In the Fall, just rock and inhale the spectacular autumn hues
Watch children dressed in costumes calling out their
Halloween, "BOO's"*

*Winter is a blanket of white glistening snow. From the porch
Christmas carols can be heard as the moon casts its glow*

*With Spring comes a new beginning that you both hear and see
Relaxing on the porch one can feel completely free*

*The porch is a comfort zone for young and old. A place
where one can see the world around unfold*

Morning on the porch

by Christian Wicker Blacksburg, Virginia

The sun only now rising
Morning awakening, the chirping birds and gurgling creek
Horses chase and play in the grassy meadows
Joyous with the breeze
The smell of fresh morning dew
The feeling of awakening, happy for the day
I await impatiently tomorrow's sunrise

Antonia Walker, Missouri Summer, 4' x 6', Oil on canvas

Porch in Big Stone Gap

by Adriana Trigiani New York City

When the spring comes,
pink and yellow tulips dance in the garden
we stay on the porch and watch the rain fill their cups

When summer arrives, the orange trumpet vines embroider
the gray trellis like silk threads on velvet
we sit on the porch as the sun comes up
and watch the bees drink from the horns

When fall passes through and there is no green
the leaves have faded to brown wool, and the
coffee colored mountains disappear behind the mist
we wait on the porch for the schoolbus

When winter settles in and the night comes
cold blue air surrounds the moon that fills us with
silver light
from our porch the universe has no seams or edges
just stars
pink glitter on black paper
a sky to write on
a dream to imagine
a porch where anything is possible.

Editor's note: In addition to being the best-selling author of *Big Stone Gap* and *Big Cherry Holler*, Adriana Trigiani is an award-winning playwright, television writer, and documentary filmmaker.

I am a porch

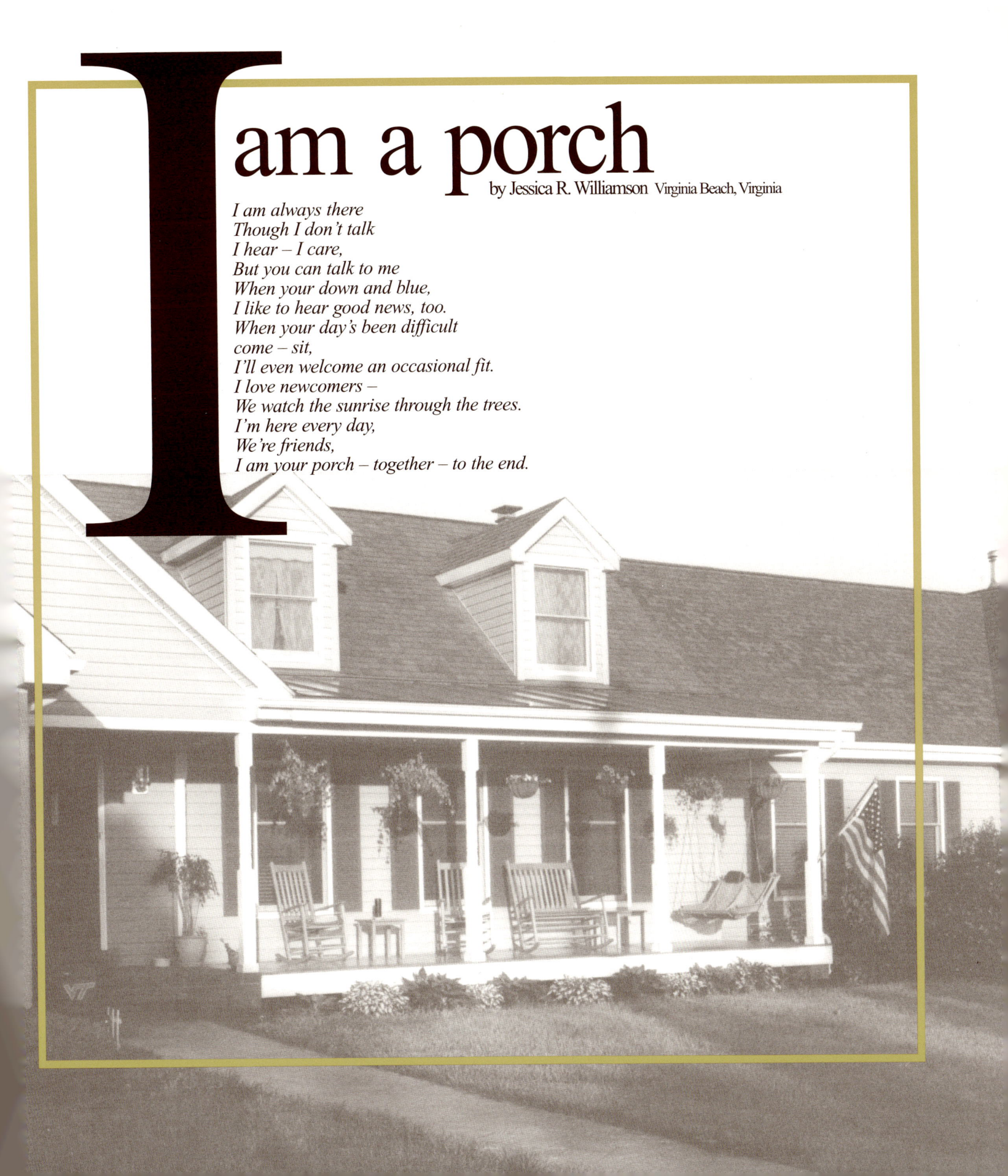

by Jessica R. Williamson Virginia Beach, Virginia

I am always there
Though I don't talk
I hear – I care,
But you can talk to me
When your down and blue,
I like to hear good news, too.
When your day's been difficult
come – sit,
I'll even welcome an occasional fit.
I love newcomers –
We watch the sunrise through the trees.
I'm here every day,
We're friends,
I am your porch – together – to the end.

My front porch

Our house was a 1940ish Cape Cod in a quiet older neighborhood in Arlington, Virginia. The sidewalk led up to big wide concrete steps bordered on both sides by large square cement pedestals, perfect for cats and kids to sun themselves. The large front porch had planked wooden floorboards that were painted a shiny battleship gray. On one end of the porch was the traditional porch swing and the other end had an old wicker sofa and lots and lots of my moms potted plants. She had a green thumb. I don't.

We sat on the porch spring, summer, fall and sometimes even in the winter. The swing was the favorite place and many times had to be replaced after falling because too many rowdy kids were piled on it, ferociously swinging. There were only three of us girls, but we always had friends around, enough to keep the swing well used. Later, when we were dating, the porch swing was a place to get away without really being away. I remember one particularly stern talk my father had with my boyfriend and me while we were on the swing, and my dad sat opposite us on a chair. It was a very embarrassing warning about what we could and could not do! We agreed to everything, but also nothing.

We had lots of cats over the years who would drag squirrels, birds, mice and moles up on the porch, usually right in front of the door as an offering before finishing their meal, leaving some portion of gut, tail or head for us to step on.

I watched the seasons come and go
Pondered all the rain and snow
Waved good-bye and said hello
I sat on the steps and cried
Waiting for my school bus ride
Sometimes going back inside

If I could bring back the years
Bury all my fears
Dry up all my tears and hug my family dears
Sit on that swing again
And visit all my kin
What a joy that would bring, what a prize to win
To be on that old front porch again

by Lucille Dowell Stephens City, Virginia

Porches Now & Then

Joyce Bupp
Mary Ann Dzama
Nan Joseph Forbes
Joan & Doug Corderman
Margaret Armstrong
Bobbie Wright Massie
Sue Gregg
Pam Hayba
Linda Ankrum
Joyce McClinden
Senator Bill Mims
Susanne & John Moliere
Patsy Potts Props
Johanna Venema
Eric & Barbara Zimmerman
Senator Charles Waddell
Evelyn Johnson
Robert & Lynn McCann

"My current house has a front porch. I can sit on the porch swing, the glider, or other chairs. The roof protects me from the outside elements, but I can still hear the sound of birds, watch the branches sway, feel the wind, and see the neighbors walking by. It gives me an introduction, since it encourages them to stop and visit. I have one neighbor, who is handicapped, but he faithfully walks his dog by my front porch daily. Another works for a laboratory and helps find solutions for diseases. One neighbor works with McGruff the dog that represents "Taking a bite out of crime." Still another is a telecommunications specialist and has a young son, so both love to come by the house and show me the son's development. It is wonderful to watch a baby, discover locomotion. Now he can pedal his tricycle and see the world beyond my porch. I look forward to many years here on my porch and the discovery of new friends who drop in, plus following the developments of my young neighbors. It is comfortable."

Clarence Hoop Springfield, Virginia

"Growing up I observed many porches, since my dad was a chaplain in the U. S. Air Force and we traveled around the world. However, the really comfortable porch was at my grandparents in West Virginia. You could come back from England, Labrador, Hawaii, Montana, and many other places, the porch would be the same with its big round posts holding up the roof, the porch swing hanging from the ceiling, other chairs scattered around, and the soothing green paint on everything. When I was younger it was a place to play with my tinker toys and vehicles I had gotten in other places. My grandfather, who died at the age of 85, was still the youngest person I ever knew and lived behind that porch. He would be with me at whatever age I was. Early on he helped me understand how to make a sled go down the hill faster. Later as I would sit on the porch for the normal weekend activity of watching guys drive by in their trucks to impress the girls, he would help me better understand what a girl was and why I would want one. These and many other instances made that porch an important place for me to discover life."

On being a farm wife . . .

Lancaster, Pennsylvania

Most food-related establishments have walk-in refrigerators. Then there are some with walkout refrigerators. Of course, our walk out refrigerator is fully functional only during certain periods of the year, that time span when outside temperatures hang at subfreezing. It saw extra heavy use during the recent holiday, when the seasonal excess of food preparations and 'feast' leftovers overflowed normal storage space.

Snow and sleet discourages the usual feline back porch perchers while a couple of wire mesh lawn chairs, lingering from summer, offers off-floor storage with surrounding cold air flow. A layer of snow only helps further chill the large roasting pan filled with turkey carcass bones and bits to be reprocessed into soup, secured for good measure inside a large, new plastic trash bag.

Additional leftovers in sealed containers add to the porch-refrigerator stash, tucked away in a sturdy, closed, cardboard box. Regular picnic coolers work equally well, especially for longer-term storage of items like quantities of citrus fruits or apples and look way more professional.

Temporary food storage is but one of the uses of our back porch which doubles as our outdoor living area in gentler weather. Most of our meals are enjoyed there, overlooking the fields, meadow and ponds. And, on suffocating July nights, we've been known to camp out on deck chairs to escape the brick-oven effect of an old brick house exposed to a stretch of 95 degree days.

Having always lived in houses with porches makes it hard for me to even imagine not having the escape hatch of an outdoor room. The most mundane jobs, from folding laundry to snapping beans from the garden, seem less of a chore when done in the fresh air ambiance of the porch. No matter what the source of the stress of the moment, five minutes on the porch provides a quick 'mental health' escape.

The wide front porch of the house where I grew up lingers on in a significant role in my childhood memories. Countless summertime vacation hours were whiled away on the porch swing of our family home, reading the likes of Nancy Drew and Tom Sawyer, or practicing embroidery or knitting. My brothers and I played games and cards there, perched on its steps to observe the farming activities of the neighborhood and used it as 'home-base' for after dark games of hide-and-seek and kick-the-can.

Both Mom and Dad, in their retirement years, spent hours and hours on their porch, entertained by the endless parade of vehicles and the comings and goings in their busy neighborhood.

In the BC (Before Computers) time of our farm years, I often lugged the accounting paperwork out to the back porch on pleasant days, weighting down bills and receipts with the stapler or edge of the accounting journal. More than once, a receipt had to be retrieved when a gust of wind whipped around the edge of the porch and sailed it out over the banister rail and into the lawn below. Laptop computers now allow for a return to the porch for paperwork on steamy days when staying inside is intolerable.

News that our second and third generations would be returning from a decade in the West coincided with our musings several springs ago about extending the porch to include a deck. It now provides an appropriate racetrack area for tricycles and riding tractors, a shady haven for a storybook moment and picnic tables which double as an impromptu tent structure when covered with old blankets.

For whatever reason, porches fell out of favor for many years, and builders erected homes minus these wonderful relaxation areas. But porches seem to be growing in popularity again, as homeowners rediscover their pleasures.

And they're a lot handier for temporarily storing a turkey carcass than just stuffing the pan in a snow bank where it might be frozen fast for weeks.

Joyce Bupp Lancaster, Pennsylvania

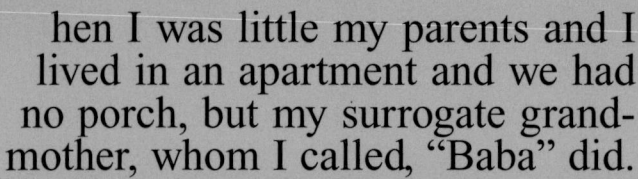

When I was little my parents and I lived in an apartment and we had no porch, but my surrogate grandmother, whom I called, "Baba" did. (My real grandparents lived in Slovakia — I never met them). I lived in a small steeltown* and my happy memories are being with people who accepted me as a family member despite no real blood family ties. Baba was a kind, patient person who loved to have company. She lived in one of the triplex houses right across the street from the church. So on most Sunday mornings, around 9 am, spring, summer and fall, we'd go to the early Mass and afterwards head over to Baba's for coffee or milk and cookies. The kids weren't allowed to have the coffee, but I can remember the delicious aroma that filled the house. I think you could smell it as soon as you hit the small front porch.

There was no discussion about it, but the adults, usually fifteen in all, gathered around in the kitchen and the kids took over the porch. It had only a metal glider and two wicker chairs so most of us, her seventeen 'grandchildren,' sat on the steps or the porch to 'people watch' the folks going to the later Mass. The girls would notice the church-goer's hats and shoes or discuss the weather, while the boys discussed the game of the season. That's when there were distinct seasons for basketball, baseball and football. Somehow I only recall the guys talking about the Pirates baseball team and the Steelers football team.

Another nice thing that I remember is that Sundays meant no stores were open so we had plenty of time to visit with our family, friends and neighbors. We'd often see people walking by and we knew or recognized everyone. It was a safe feeling, and I guess you could say life was not so harried then.

The majority of those adults have died, and all of us children have grown up. The steel mill has long gone and the church moved to a new site. We (the children) moved out of that town, so I have no idea if any of the others have a front porch now. I live in a small development and have a very small porch, but rarely sit outside. Hardly anyone walks by. And the few that do, I don't know. How times have changed!

Mary Anne Dzama Fairfax, Virginia

*Author's Note: *The steeltown referred to is, Aliquippa, in western Pennsylvania. It was headquarters for the Jones & Laughlin Steel Co. and the town was named after the Queen of the Delaware Indian Tribe who originally lived in that area. Supposedly Queen Aliquippa traded with William Penn.*

Dear Sir,

Enclosed is a picture of our home on Main Street. The porches are an integral part of the house, the west porch has been used for parties, Sunday suppers, etc. The east porch has an old swing great for summer evenings. The front porch is classic with big wooden benches.

    Come Look!

                      Nan Joseph Forbes, Purcellville, Virginia

Longview farm,

near Leesburg, Virginia, the home of **Joan and Doug Corderman** was built in 1903. Its fieldstone porch is raised to allow the foxhunters a 'stirrup cup' on their mounts. Old lanterns flank the front door surrounded by boxwoods and classical columns commanding a view of the rolling fields and woods beyond. Residents of Longview still watch the Loudoun Hunt gallop across the fields. Barn cats sleep lazily on porch chairs, while frogs and crickets from the nearby pond provide a summer's evening symphony.

Lovettsville Porch

There is a porch located on the Armstrong Family Farm outside of Lovettsville, Virginia. It overlooks the Dutchman's Creek. The house was built in the early 1800s and has always had this front porch. The Armstrongs have owned it for over fifty years. "It is a wonderful place to sit alone and read a good book, watch the birds migrate south, or just listen to the creek. It is even a better place for family and friends to gather."

Margaret Armstrong

Bobbie Wright Massie remembers...

When I was little,

I thought the fire escape to our apartment in New York was a porch. You couldn't put stuff on it though and the only time you could go out on it was when no one was looking. If you did go out on it, somebody's mother called your mother to tell. Then there was trouble. I missed the farm in Bedford County, Virginia, and my grandmother's porch while we lived in the city.

My Daddy's father built the house and all the buildings around it just about the time my Daddy was born. A fire burned away part of the old brick house in the orchard. The farm's schoolhouse porch looked right at the porch of the new house. My grandfather died the year I was born, so I only know about him from pictures.

My Daddy is the little boy in the picture of all the family on the steps of the porch between the columns. There is a small pair of shoes on the step that I think belonged to Daddy's baby sister. I think she is sucking her thumb and is sitting on Grandfather's lap in the back row. Grandmother is next to them, but isn't looking at them. The sister in the white blouse won a beauty contest once. Her husband is in the picture with her. Grandmother did not like the beauty contest thing. One other sister in the front looks about Daddy's age. All the other sisters and Daddy's brother look like they are grown ups. Nobody looks too happy. I hate their clothes. I can't imagine doing anything fun in them. My grandfather's sister and her husband are there, too. I don't know anything about them. When people visit, they still take pictures on that porch. I wish we had some pictures of my great grandfather's house in the orchard. I don't know if it had a porch.

The porch at my grandmother's house at the farm was big. You couldn't leave stuff on it either, not even in the chairs or on the swing. She wanted it clean and not messy. She said it was the first thing people saw when they drove down the lane. "What kind of people would they think lived in this house, if there were dirt and trash?" I never answered. Nobody ever answered my grandmother unless it was the same thing she said.

my Grandmother

my Grandfather

The Wright Family c 1914

my Daddy

My grandmother's porch had four columns. I could barely get my arms around one when I was really little. If you fell off the porch while you were spinning, it could hurt a lot. There were so many steps down to the ground. Mama made me wash my face and comb my hair if someone took a picture of us on the steps. I usually sat on the bottom step at my Daddy's feet.

I learned a lot on my grandmother's porch. I learned that you had to sweep it everyday even if it weren't dirty. I learned not to trust grown ups, especially if it was your Daddy. Most important I learned that it felt really good to get back at somebody who had been mean to you, especially if it was your big sister. I learned the spanking was worth it afterwards, too.

There was no smoking allowed on my grandmother's porch. When Daddy or Mama wanted a cigarette they would walk down the road toward the creek, or go behind one of the other buildings.

my Grandfather *my Grandmother*

The Wright Family circa 1932
Same porch same folks

my Daddy
William Wright

When I was little, *cont.*

I learned to watch out for what grownups say because Daddy couldn't smoke on that front porch. Even if grandmother had gone to town, she would know when she walked onto the porch if Daddy had smoked a cigarette there.

My Daddy seemed like a city daddy in the city and a country daddy at the farm. One morning, I heard him talking on the porch with some old friends. No one was smoking. Even Daddy's friends did not smoke on grandmother's porch. When I walked outside I saw a piece of chocolate candy on the first step down off the porch next to Daddy. I asked him if I could I have a piece? "Don't take too big a bite," he answered, and I did take too big a bite. Then they all laughed, even my Daddy, while I spit and spit and spit. It burned my tongue. It smelled and tasted terrible and I thought I was sick. Mama was mad at Daddy for a while. She thought that chewing tobacco was very bad for children and I did too and still do. Daddy never told me he was sorry. Nobody told grandmother.

I think the best time I ever had on my grandmother's porch was when my big sister got Deanna Durbin paper dolls. My big sister has the same Daddy as me, but a different mother. Everyone says my big sister is very pretty and nice. She isn't so nice to me. My cousin is exactly my age. My sister let my cousin play with the Deanna Durbin paper dolls, but would not let me. My sister said I was too little and I would tear them.

My big sister broke grandmother's rule. She left the paper doll book, cut outs, and scissors on the steps of the porch. It was a sunny day and there was no one on the porch, in the yard or in the school house. So I sat in the sunshine and took my time and cut the paper dolls and the book into little pieces. My sister got a new Deanna Durbin paper dolls and I got a spanking. I was supposed to tell my sister that I was sorry. I didn't. They did tell my grandmother.

Sometimes I swing on the porch by myself and pretend children are running down the stairs of the school house porch across the yard right past the front porch. The front porch outside was like the parlor was inside then. It was for company and special things. Daddy and his brother and sisters used the back porch after school where there were benches for their stuff, especially muddy shoes.

When I sit on the front porch steps I can see almost all the way to the churchyard where my Grandfather is buried. The fields between the porch and the churchyard are part of the farm. Sometimes they are like gold. They always are quiet. I guess my grandfather watches us and his home place, and we watch him from the porch he built.

Bobbie Wright Massie Atlantic, North Carolina

Bobbie Wright Massie c 2005

A Lincoln Porch History

The date 1891 is carved into a brick in one of the two chimneys in the attic of the house on Lincoln Road, and is assumed by the present generations of Greggs to be the year the house was constructed by Mrs. Eliza Rawson, who herself had an interesting life and background.

Mrs. Rawson died in 1907. Her sons rented it to a family named Cole who used it as a summer boarding house until 1915 when Mr. & Mrs. Edward Buntley Gregg bought it. Mrs. Holmes Gregg, the wife of their now deceased son, daughter Susan and family, live with her part time.

The Gregg house has had numerous changes, large and small over the years. The latest, in the summer of 2001, the porches were added to the 1930 addition which combined three rooms: the kitchen, small dining area and a sofa area with a large picture window, into one. The dining area does not replace the main dining room and the living room of the original house. We are now looking forward to another summer on the porches.

Sue Gregg Lincoln, Virginia

When I first saw the cabin in 1982, I think it was the front porch that charmed us.

I envisioned myself sitting on a swing, nursing my babies (we didn't have any children yet) or rocking them to sleep in an old rocker. It had to have been the porch that influenced us because the rest of the house was awful — no electricity, no plumbing!

As a matter of fact, the log cabin, built about 250 years ago, had been abandoned for years and even had cattle roaming through it because the doors were missing. It was sold to a contractor on the courthouse steps at auction for back taxes. The contractor decided the cabin was a hopeless project and he chose to sell it, but first, he fixed the porch. I do believe that without the porch, we wouldn't have taken a second look at the cabin. Anyway, we are blessed with five children and each of them was rocked on that porch. Unlike many homes, our front door is the door we use exclusively, so that means every coming and going includes crossing the porch. Leaving home heavily pregnant, then returning with a baby. The first days of school and so many days I sat on the swing waiting for the school bus to bring the children home. There are memories of anxiously waiting on the porch for a favorite visitor, often Grandma, and now one of the older children returning home.

The author/journalist and Virginia native, Russell Baker grew up in this cabin. After he won the Pulitzer Prize for his novel *Growing Up*, people came by and asked questions. He told me his earliest memories dated from the time his younger sister, Doris was born here in this cabin.

Doris and Russell Baker, circa 1931

I've learned over the years, there are many amusing stories associated with the cabin. For example, many people have stopped by to warn us that it was haunted. They couldn't believe that we were actually not afraid to live here. One story I heard was confirmed recently: A man died upstairs but since he lived alone he wasn't discovered for a few days. Because of his prone position in death, it was impossible to carry him down the narrow twisting stairway. So, a hole was cut in the ceiling to lower him through. He was then carried out across the porch.

Pam Hayba Morrisonville, Virginia

That's me with my
father, Barney Boockoff
on our porch steps in
Collingswood,
New Jersey 1951.

Me and my dog,
Rex 1953.

That's me in the middle with our neighbor Annie, on my right and my big sister Jane Marguerite sitting on our front stoop in Philadelphia 1949.

Recently, I went back to visit my old house in Philly...the first time in over 40 years. It looked just the same.

Linda Boockoff Ankrum

"There is nothing like a front porch.

We use ours from early spring to late fall. Ours is like an outdoor living room. We have grass mats on the floor, comfortable wicker furniture, lots of pillows, plants and even a porch swing. The street in front of our porch — very little traffic. So many of our neighbors walk their dogs and teach their kids how to ride bicycles. Most people stop, talk, join us for a drink, it's a great way to get in touch with everyone in our small town. Some evenings we get out of the air-conditioning and sit there in the dark, talk and watch the fireflies. It's nice to have early morning coffee there. Porches are wonderful places to relax, socialize and meditate.

Get one!"

Jocelyn Mclinden Hillsboro, Virginia

Photographs: Hugh & Jocelyn McLinden's porch with Timothy, Kendall, Lauren & their dog Daisy.

Illustration: The Vance House, Hillsboro, by Dana B. Thompson '97

Lathan and Shirley Mims, parents of Senator Bill Mims, on their Harrisonburg, Virginia porch

I grew up in Harrisonburg, Virginia, in a late Victorian house on a busy residential street. On many summer evenings, my grandmother and my parents and I would sit on the front porch and 'watch the world go by.' In fact, I learned to count, in part, by counting cars from my spot on the porch. Many of my best childhood memories involved that porch, in some manner.

When my wife and I were looking at houses for sale in Eastern Loudoun in 1987, we found one in Countryside with a wrap-around porch that reminded me of my childhood home, although it is on a cul-de-sac instead of a busy street.

As my wife occasionally notes...

"We bought the porch – it's fortunate that a house is attached!"

Senator Bill Mims Countryside, Virginia

"**We** think our front porch is one of the best features of our home. Many hours are spent there with our dogs, just reading, rocking, bird watching or reflecting. Of course the spectacular views of our country side help make it so special."

Susanne & John P. Moliere Purcellville, Virginia

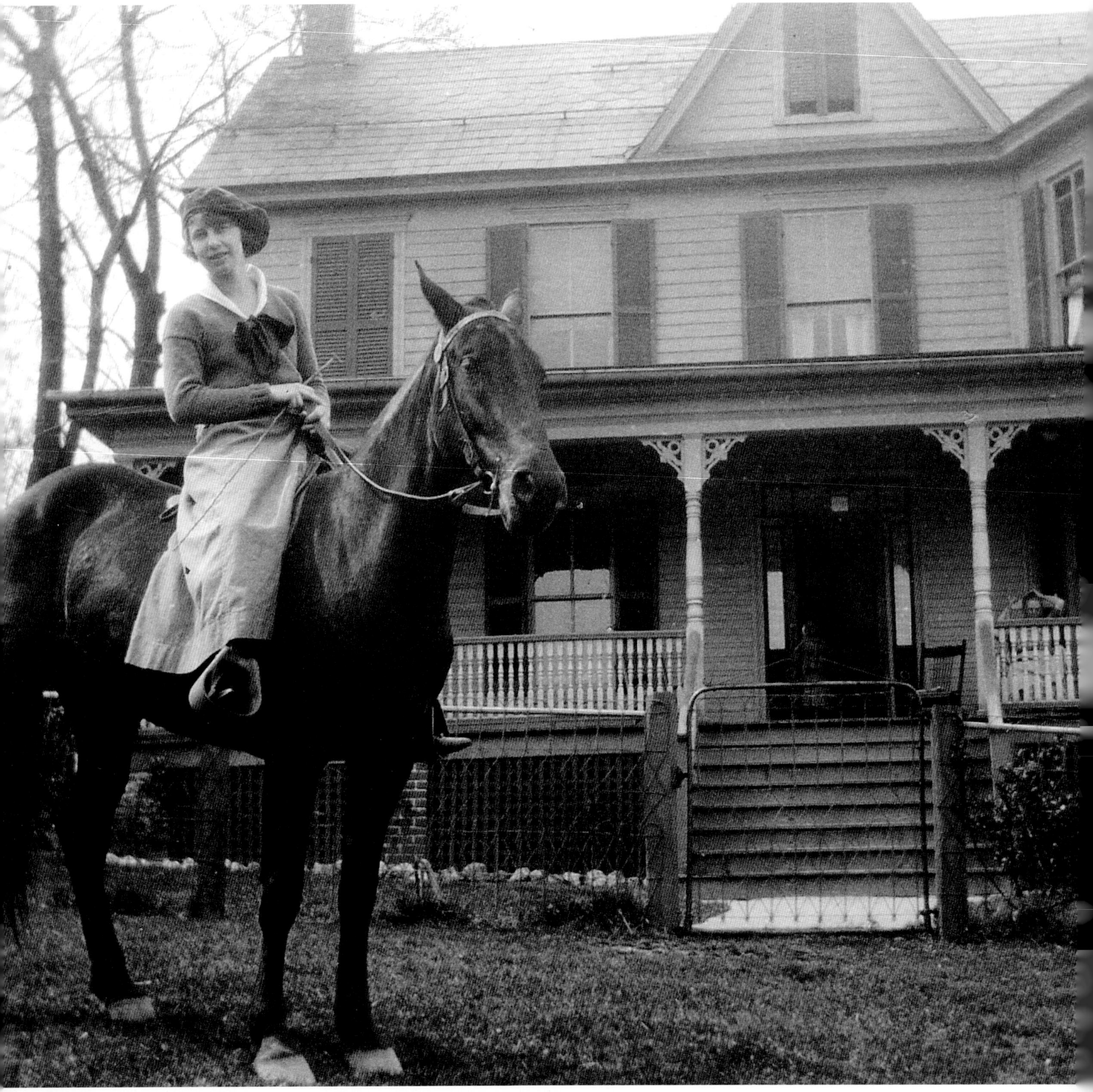

the Potts Farm, Orchard Crest

was established in 1747 along the Blue Ridge mountains by David Potts of Bucks County, Pennsylvania. The original homestead and house on Potts Lane was the site of a two-story log cabin that was renovated in 1900 and a front porch added by Clinton Potts and his sons Thurston and Jennings. The sons are pictured with their sisters in 1914 in front of the porch in the photo (on next page). Nine generations have lived on the original land grant from Lord Fairfax, and it has been an active farming operation for over 250 years. Currently it operates as a Grade A Dairy with a one hundred Holstein cow milking herd. Edwin Clinton, Edwin Clinton Jr. and grandson, Justin Clinton Potts are managing the farming operation.

Marty Koch Potts   Orchard Crest Farm, Purcellville, Virginia

Photo: Loudelle Hale Potts on her horse, Rowdy c1912

Porch Memories

When I was a child, our house had three porches and each had a different use. The back porch had a concrete floor with three steps leading to the sidewalk. The door that entered the utility room from the back porch had a screen door that was the only door that was closed most of the summer. Only when the weather was cold did the wooden door get closed.

The back porch was where everyone entered the house, even guests. It faced the driveway and was the most convenient. It had the usual doormat and broom but there was also a cardboard box with old worn out shirts lining the bottom, which was for the cats to sleep in. Since I lived on a farm, there was an abundance of cats and kittens. In the cold weather usually three or four cats slept in a big pile in the box. When I took cat food out on the porch each morning there were usually six or seven cats waiting for their breakfast. In the summer the cats would climb the screen door to get someone's attention. They usually wanted to come in the house and a few special cats were allowed.

In the corner of the porch was a barrel, which contained the empty food cans and unburnable trash. And a few feet from the barrel was a covered bucket, which held the kitchen food scraps. This sat near the front edge of the porch so that it could easily be picked up and taken to the manure spreader to be emptied. Often my father was the one to empty the 'slop bucket' as he went to the barn but I can remember a few times that I was sent to empty it, too. The barrel and the "slop bucket" did not add to the beauty of the porch but they were necessities.

In the winter, after we kids had been riding our sleds down the steep hill behind the old barn, we dragged our sleds back to the house and dropped them wherever – often one was leaning against the back porch. Our sleds usually stayed there until our father or mother insisted that we put them away in the shop where they belonged.

The back porch was even used as part of a makeshift kitchen in the 1960s when my parents had the kitchen remodeled. The remodeling was done in the summer of a year that was a drought year, which was helpful for the remodeling process and for the temporary kitchen on the porch. The kitchen was unusable during remodeling. One exterior wall was torn out – no plumbing and the floor torn up. The room was gutted. My mother used the sink in the downstairs bathroom as her kitchen sink, a hot plate was on the counter in the utility room and the kitchen table was put in there. The refrigerator and electric stove were put on the back porch where they were hooked up and used. My mother remembers that my aunt, uncle and cousins from Georgia came for a visit that summer and she cooked the big mid-day meals for the family and visiting relatives at the stove on the back porch. As a child, this was fun. As an adult, I cannot imagine trying to cook big farm meals with this set up.

Our house also had a screened-in-porch. It joined the back porch at the corner and the living room could be entered from this porch. The wooden floor was painted porch-floor blue and I can faintly remember the porch before the screen was put on. It had wide wooden steps leading to the yard. When the screen was put around the sides of the porch, the wooden steps were torn off (less maintenance) and the porch was entered from a cement slab that connected the back porch and this screened-in-porch.

For seating there were several lawn chairs and even a chair that reclined. This was my favorite. When we had company in the summer, Mom would bar-b-que chicken on the grill and we would eat on the screened-in-porch. As we prepared for the meal, we would pass the dishes and food out the den window, which opened onto the porch. This shortened the number of steps that it would take to walk around to the door. The den part of the house was built of log and so the windowsills were very deep. These deep sills made great places to set the items that needed to go to the porch and the person on the porch could take them out of the sill and place them on the card table.

This porch also contained a collection of plants that my sister, my mother and I all contributed to. There were spider plants, begonias, snake plants, impatiens and other plants that people gave us.

Our garden was very large by today's standards. My mother froze lots of vegetables to be used in the winter. In June when the peas were ready, my mother would start early in the morning, after breakfast was cleaned up and pick peas. She would have to stop to fix the noonday meal and if there were lots of peas ready at once, she would pick in the hot afternoon sun. I did not pick very many peas. I think my sister helped more with that, but I was the lucky one who sat on the cool screened-in porch and shelled peas. There were brown paper grocery bags full of peas that needed shelling. I held the peas that needed shelling on a piece of newspaper in my lap and dumped the shelled peas on this newspaper, too. On the floor beside me was a bag in which to throw the empty pods. When I had all of the peas in my lap shelled, I would dump the shelled peas in a large pan or bowl and get the next bunch of unshelled peas out of the bag. I remember shelling for half of the afternoon but I enjoyed this. Usually there was more than one person shelling, and it was a great time to talk. Sometimes my grandmother drove to the farm in the afternoon and helped shell. Friends who happened to come to visit also helped. When my mother finished picking, she shelled too. At times there were three or four of us shelling. As we shelled we laughed at the few stray peas that popped out of the pods and bounced across the porch floor. One of us would eventually have to collect the ones that had escaped. Occasionally, we sat on the porch and shelled peas during thunderstorms. I remember the sudden and welcome temperature change that the storms brought. I also remember a few lightning strikes and rolls of thunder that seemed a bit too close but in most cases, we just moved our chairs further away from the edge so that we wouldn't get wet.

The third porch on our house was the front porch. It was the usual early 1900s-style porch that extended across the front of the house with a wooden floor, white columns and railings, and a wide set of steps leading to the shady front yard which was full of mature maple trees. The living room had a bay window that took some of the space from one end of the porch. On summer evenings when the fireflies were out, my brother, my sister and I would get an old jar from the cellar, punch holes in the metal lid and catch lightening bugs. When it was almost bedtime, we would take the jar up on the porch and show it to our parents and watch the bugs light up in the darkness. We released the bugs before going in the house to bed.

My father enjoyed playing the coronet and sometimes after supper on a summer evening when the sun was going down, he would take his coronet out on the front porch and play taps. It had a very haunting sound and I'm sure the sound drifted to the neighboring farms in the stillness of the evening.

On one end of the porch was a porch swing. It was so much fun for kids but probably a headache for my mother. When the cousins came to visit, we would have one or two kids in the swing and the other would push the swing as high as we dared and either jump onto the swing or jump out of the way. The swing would go fast and high and would go back just far enough to get a little slack in the chains so that we bumped as we swung down. We laughed and got a little careless and had to be told not to swing so high or someone would get hurt. We spent a lot of time playing on the porch swing.

My cousins from Georgia and I were swinging, giggling and jumping in and out of the swing on the front porch one summer day when my mother and my Aunt Peggy were in the garden picking green beans. From the porch we heard Aunt Peggy scream. Of course we went to find out what had happened. As Aunt Peggy was picking beans, she was pushing what she thought was a garden hose out of her way as she picked down the row. Finally, when she got to the end of the hose she found that it was a black snake! I cannot remember if she picked any more beans that day.

In 1973, after my brother, Eddie's wedding to Marty Koch, my parents invited friends and relatives back to our house for supper. It was June, and we ate on the front porch. There were so many people that we were sitting on the chairs, on the porch steps, and were leaning against the railings. Everyone was laughing and talking, and I remember that I was sitting on the porch with my feet on the top step talking to Janice Frame when the phone rang. When my father came back out on the porch after answering the phone, he said that it was my brother calling to say that he and his bride had arrived at their honeymoon destination safely. There were several remarks from the group about calling home for fatherly advice. We all laughed and enjoyed each other's company until after dark.

Patsy Potts Props Mt. Solon, Virginia

October 2004, the wedding day of Jessica Potts & Jürgen Venema on the porch at Orchard Crest, site of 104 years of family gatherings.

My American Porch

There I was, seventeen years old, a German exchange-student with long, blond braided hair trying to understand what was going on around me, much less within me. I was sitting on the big front porch of my new home — my home for the next year at least — among my new family, my American family and their neighbors. People from next door and across the street, relatives and friends were coming over to welcome me, the young German girl, to America. Everybody seemed to be very interested in where I came from, how I became an exchange-student, and how my flight was. And, of course they all wanted to know how I liked the US and the city of Detroit, in particular.

Let me tell you the story:

In the fall of 1962, when I was in the 10th grade of a German Gymnasium (high-school, college-prep courses only) my homeroom teacher recommended me to apply for a student exchange program. For many years, one out of every two students from our school spent a school year in the USA. So I knew there could be a chance to participate in this unique experience, but never really believed that I would be the one chosen some day.

I sent my application to the *Deutsches Youth for Understanding Komitee* and was invited to come to an interview in Oldenburg about a one-hour train ride from home. I remember very well the building and the room I had to go to. I was accepted and had to attend a workshop to be prepared for life as an exchange student.

The months before I left were filled with excitement and anxiety. In my dreams I was already living in my future environment, but this idea scared me so much, I didn't want to go. But then, events propelled me along and, suddenly I was there, in America. After the long plane ride of more than 20 hours, every time I sat down I felt as if I were still flying. Yes, it really took that long from Amsterdam to Detroit with stops in Ireland and Vermont. My host family picked me up at the airport and when we arrived at their home, told me to make myself comfortable. I didn't understand what that meant, so I changed and put on another dress. I found out later they expected me to put on shorts. I had never been allowed to wear shorts back home, so I didn't have any in my suitcase. They closely watched me unpack. Their gift of welcome to me — a pair of thongs — made me look a little more American. But the very first night my family took me shopping for shorts and blouses that adjusted at least my appearance.

Back then, in August 1963, I had problems understanding the language although I had studied it in school for six years. We learned all kinds of vocabulary, but no every day expressions or slang. Sitting on the big front porch and enjoying the warm weather was very relaxing. Slowly, it sank in, I really was living in a country far away from home. But conversations and TV were extremely tiring during the first three months. Many times I did not even realize when I fell asleep. After a while I learned to do all kinds of things on the porch including homework on my lap. I know my porch is still there. Telling you about it brings back many fond memories of people and situations, which changed my life.

Johanna Venema Jemgum, Germany

the *Wrap-around* porch

of our West Main Street home was an initial attraction to the house and, nearly twenty years later, it's still a favorite spot. It's long-been said that the kitchen is the heart of a home. That being the case, a welcoming porch serves as outstretched arms of hospitality. Functioning as a visitor center, living area, potting shed, or respite from the sun, rain, or storm, it's a lovely perching spot to watch the world go by! There's no better place to take a break from snow-shoveling, cool off beneath fans after gardening, enjoy alfresco dining, or dreamily pass the day.

Barbara & Eric Zimmerman   Purcellville, Virginia

from Georgia to

Senator Charles "Charlie" Waddell

Virginia

"I am pleased to write of childhood memories of life on the porches of my native Georgia with its wealth of old southern colonial homes graced with magnificent porches. Also, later as an adult, I have memorable moments associated with the porches of Loudoun County, Virginia where I moved with my family over four decades ago.

One of my earliest memories was of family reunions where our parents and so many aunts, uncles, and cousins would gather for fellowship, socializing and lots of photo-taking sessions. One of the pictures that I treasure is of my father's family at a reunion just after my dad returned from France in WWI. My mother was there but this was before they were even married. My dad, in the picture is so handsome and my mother so beautiful, but I was always curious why they stood on opposite ends of the porch for that photograph in 1919. I never asked.

Later, as I was growing up with my brothers, we lived on a farm in an old country home with a wrap-around porch. It was a favorite place for so many activities including making home-made ice cream, cutting watermelons, churning butter, playing games and visiting with neighbors and relatives who would most times show up unannounced. This, of course, was accepted practice then because we had no telephone. It was from the porch at night where the older folks would watch us kids playing games or chasing fireflies in the front yard.

Waddell home place c1920 Jackson Trail, Georgia.

Circled, left to right:
Mother, Grandparents & Father of Charlie Waddell.

Maternal Grandparents, Thomas Washington and Rilla McEver White

Many times our grandparents sat rockin' on the porch, sometimes dipping snuff, while telling us stories about the Civil War. With their fathers off in Virginia fighting for the Confederacy, their mothers would have to hide the livestock in caves to avoid having them confiscated by Sherman's Army during his infamous march to the sea.

Another activity that I shall never forget was my father practicing his singing. Dad led the choir at Zion Baptist Church where we worshipped and he would spend hours on the front porch with his songbooks. My brothers and I would often join him because we also loved singing. Our mother would join in making it a family sing-along, something I enjoy to this day.

After WWII when my two older brothers, Myron and Ralph returned from the South Pacific, they would spend lots of time on the porch telling us stories about their experiences in the war. I was 12 and my younger brother, Leroy, 10. We were wide eyed with excitement as we sat by them on the front porch so proud to have them home after four years and willing to share their war adventures with us.

Around the age of 15, I began to date, I remember vividly getting my first kiss. We were sitting on the front porch swing of my girlfriend's house. Can't remember her name but I do remember that swing. Everyone in rural Georgia had a swing on their porch and it was so much fun spending time there while talking to family, friends and especially courting.

I left Georgia to come to Northern Virginia and work for American Airlines in Washington. But, I remember vividly returning home on vacation from my job to celebrate my 21st birthday, which included my favorite coconut cake with candles, served at my favorite spot on the front porch of my parent's home in Braselton, Georgia.

After moving to Loudoun County in the late 50s and ultimately getting into politics, many of my political events centered around porches. When I ran for County Supervisor and Virginia Senator, knocking on doors of local citizens, much of my campaign spiel took place on the front porches. I remember having a cam-

A cake from Dauphne Rouse, classmate and neighbor on their shared 21st birthday in Braselton, Georgia.

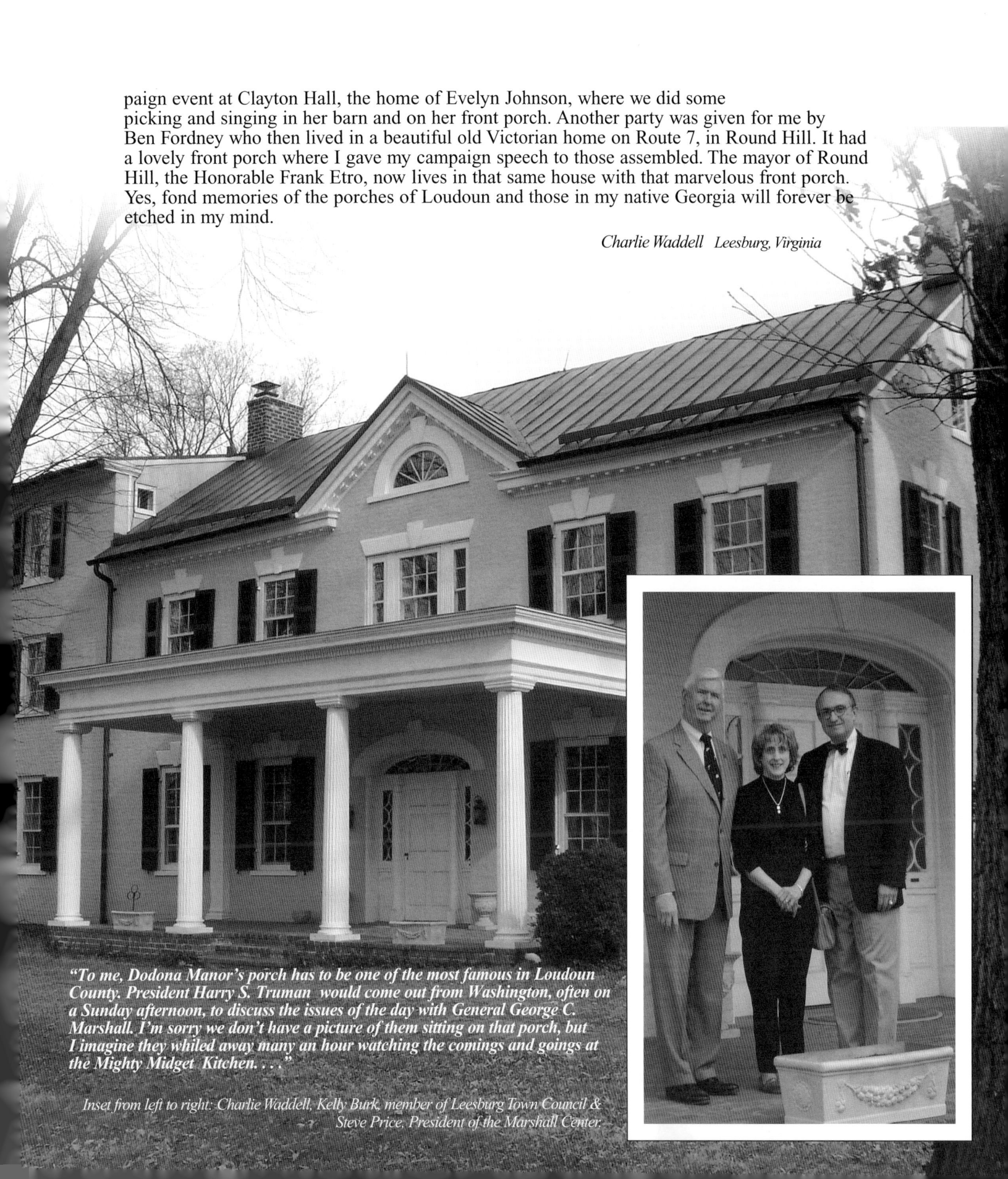

paign event at Clayton Hall, the home of Evelyn Johnson, where we did some picking and singing in her barn and on her front porch. Another party was given for me by Ben Fordney who then lived in a beautiful old Victorian home on Route 7, in Round Hill. It had a lovely front porch where I gave my campaign speech to those assembled. The mayor of Round Hill, the Honorable Frank Etro, now lives in that same house with that marvelous front porch. Yes, fond memories of the porches of Loudoun and those in my native Georgia will forever be etched in my mind.

Charlie Waddell Leesburg, Virginia

"To me, Dodona Manor's porch has to be one of the most famous in Loudoun County. President Harry S. Truman would come out from Washington, often on a Sunday afternoon, to discuss the issues of the day with General George C. Marshall. I'm sorry we don't have a picture of them sitting on that porch, but I imagine they whiled away many an hour watching the comings and goings at the Mighty Midget Kitchen...."

Inset from left to right: Charlie Waddell, Kelly Burk, member of Leesburg Town Council & Steve Price, President of the Marshall Center.

I like to tell my children, "You had an idyllic childhood." Not only did I have the privilege of living it with them, I wrote about it weekly for seventeen years as the Bluemont correspondent for the *Loudoun Times-Mirror* and *The Clarke Courier*. And a lot of their growing up in our little village of Bluemont was played out on our big front porch. The concrete floor porch had been added to the 1797 stone house in the late '30s. It has a tin roof, flat though it has never caved in from a snow accumulation. Four columns frame the facade and originally it had a formal wooden ceiling which developed a leak. One workman wanted to tear the roof off to correct the problem. Many times since, I have counted my blessings, I said "No!" We just tore out the ceiling and now with the exposed beams, it works beautifully, thank you.

In essence the front porch is our extended living space from Memorial Day to after the Bluemont Fair, the third weekend of September. The number of birthday candles lit on cakes on the picnic table could never be calculated. As part of the early celebrations of the birthdays, the daughters would put on plays with entrances and exits from the hall onto the porch. A young neighbor came on one occasion, accompanied by his two pet goats, who gleefully mounted the ledges of the wide steps, the children screaming in excitement.

Dinner parties for adult friends have graced the big sturdy picnic table, made by a a foster child in his vo-tech classes through Loudoun Valley High School.

The Porch at

There have been parties for political candidates and a fond-remembered steak dinner shared as raindrops fell on the tin roof.

The wicker and the hanging swing, bought from Nichols Hardware, go out in May. Red geraniums always decorate the ledges in window boxes.

In previous summer evenings, the children frolicked, catching lightning bugs on the lawn or sometimes helped churn ice cream for the Fourth of July celebration at the old school grounds in the village.

In fall we put out the pumpkins and stack the wood for the approaching cold, take down the swing and put out the old red school bench.

In winter, the sled and snow shovels go out. The prettiest sight I ever saw on the porch was a bough of freshly cut holly dusted with snow, an early Christmas gift from a neighbor. I have my bird house collection out on a tin-top table and there among some of my favorite things and blooming plants, I like to sit on the front porch. Feeling the cool breezes from the swing in the summer, I recall special times with family and friends. But oh, how I wish, I could once utter to a passerby as in the days of another generation, "Won't you come up and sit a spell?"
I have the porch for it!

Evelyn Porterfield Johnson Bluemont, Virginia

Clayton Hall

the Winner!

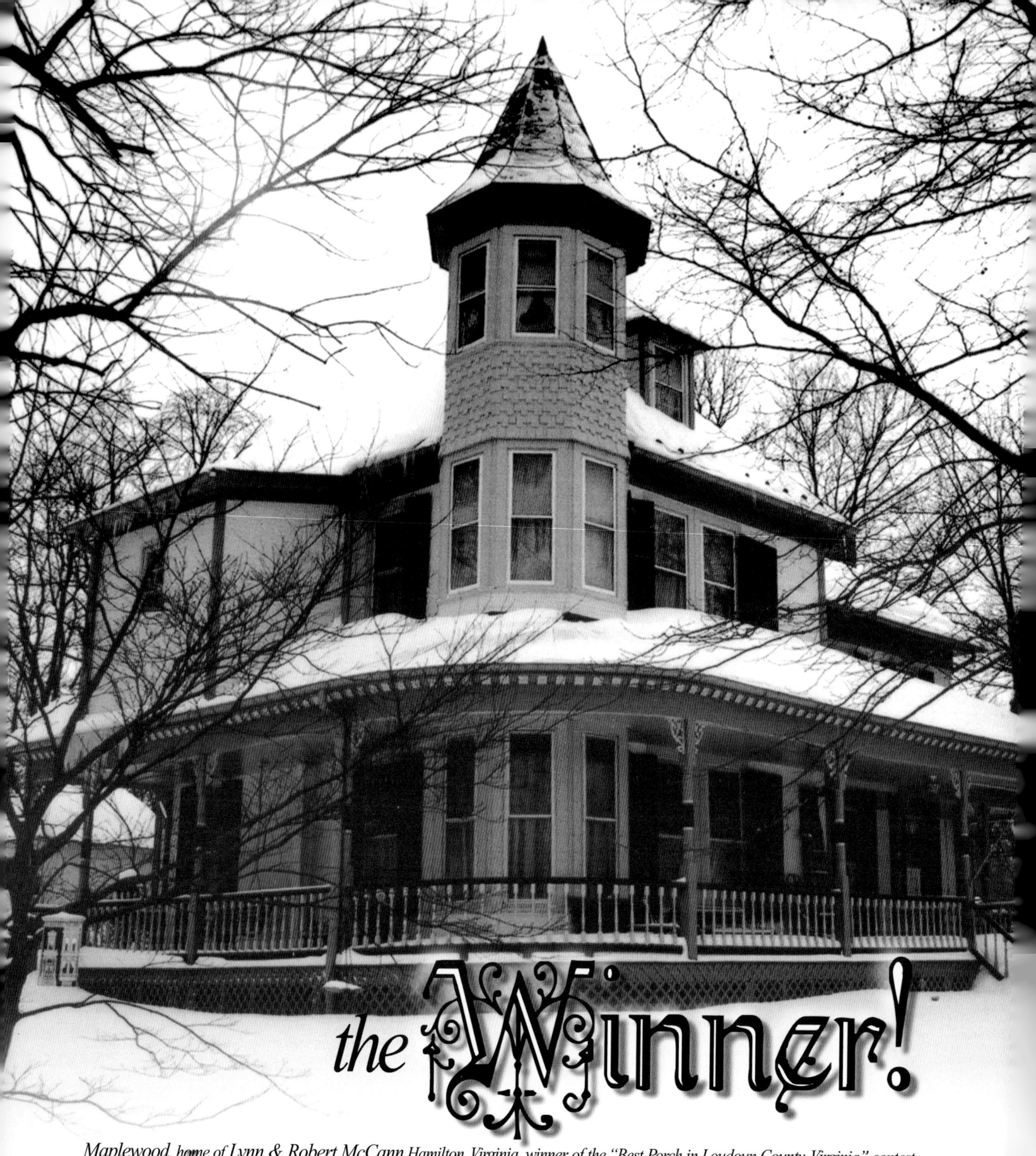

Maplewood, home of *Lynn & Robert McCann* Hamilton, Virginia, winner of the "Best Porch in Loudoun County, Virginia" contest.

Maplewood was built in at least three stages. The earliest construction dates to the late 1700s, and consists of a two-story brick structure. The 1700s portion of the house now comprises the kitchen and an adjacent family room. The construction is solid brick masonry, painted on the exterior and plastered on the interior. The family room contains an original painted wooden mantelpiece. The plain board interior door and window surrounds are also original. The 1840s section was built by Richard Ruse, a noted Hamilton carpenter and mason. The Offleys hired Barney Noland to build a Queen Anne-style addition to the front and east sides of the house in 1872. This addition included a three story bay-windowed tower and massive wrap-around porch that define the present character of the house. Interestingly, the date, 1872 is engraved on a section of plaster wall in the attic. Although several houses in Hamilton of about the same period contain towers, Maplewood's is by far the grandest in scale, and the most detailed architecturally. The tower rises a full three stories, and the tall witches cap roof gives it even greater height. The tower's second story is highlighted by rows of decorative, wood shingled siding.

In addition to the wrap-around porch, the exterior of the house is also noted for its large windows, varied rooflines, and single dormer window. The house has retained its original louvred shutters. The doors, windows and moldings are all original and are typical of the 1870s although the wooden corner blocks at the doors and windows are more detailed than was common, consisting of a central stylized flower rather than the usual bulls-eye.

On the first floor, the east parlor is unusually large. The room is divided by a large arched opening, framed by wooden protectors, which defined a small back sitting area. The two parlor areas are served by back-to-back fireplaces set at an angle. The smaller has a simple wooden mantelpiece, with circular applied moldings. The larger part of the room boasts a more ornate mantelpiece, with applied swag molding, tiled surround and tiled floor. According to Offley family history, the Offley's used the family sitting area during the late 1890s when reduced circumstances forced them to open the rest of the house to boarders.

The front parlor opens onto a central hall that features a lovely staircase, with large turned newel post, turned balusters and walnut rail. The wall beneath the stairs on the first floor is covered by a full height paneling with an applied ogee molding. The first floor west parlor contains unusual windows that open onto the front porch. The sashes are narrow, double hung one-over-one in style, but below them are paneled wood sections hinged to open inward. These doors are called 'coffin-doors' in local parlance, and were supposedly used as the name suggests, to allow a coffin to be taken in or out of the house when funerals were conducted from the home.

The second floor is noted for the unusual curved doorways that define the staircase landing. One wall contains decorative bedboard molding. Two bedrooms open off the landing; the larger is defined by the bay windows of the tower.

The original wrap-around porch fell into disrepair, and was removed during the 1940s. The McCann's, the current owners, have restored the wrap-around porch, using photographs of the house taken between 1913 and 1929 by the Offley family. The restoration included reproducing the elegant turned posts and Eastlake-style decorative wooden brackets. Although the porch originally did not have railing installed, the McCann's added a rail for safety reasons for their young son. They acquired the rails and balusters from a house, c1895, that was being demolished in Strasburg, Virginia. That porch was 100-feet long, a perfect match for their 92-foot porch. Other restoration projects over the last four years have included the rebuilding and re-pointing of all three chimneys, museum quality restoration of all the cornices, soffets and the replacement of old and battered walkways with brick.

A SUGGESTED DESIGN FOR A STUDENT-BUILT PORCH AT LOUDOUN VALLEY HIGH SCHOOL

by Michael Dolan

Contributors:

Amendment One
Leesburg Today

Better Impressions

Priscilla Godfrey

Sue Gregg

Evelyn Johnson

Loudoun County
 Public Schools

Loudoun Valley High School
 Endowment Fund

George & Austin Miller

Reflections/Millie Gallahan

State Farm Insurance/
 Mike Perry

The Waltonians

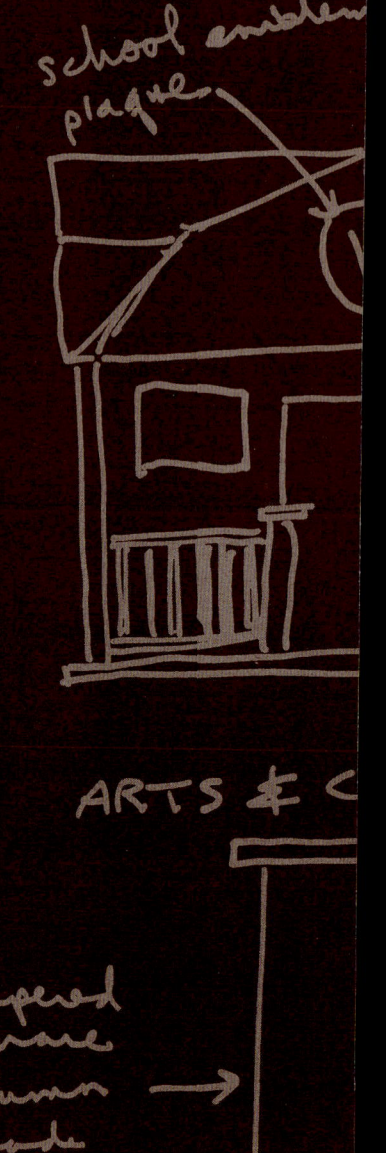

Other books from

**dancingink
press**

Sheets to the Wind 1998

Paeonian to Paris 2000

Sheets for Men Only 2005

Vive la Soupe! 2006

*Paris to Paeonian
with Fresh Eyes* 2006

Contact:
dancingink@aol.com

Mr. & Mrs. David Neer & family; Jessie, Mabel, Nathan & Edwin Hillsboro, Virginia c1900.